Jim Grindlay

CW00734800

BRITISH RAILWAYS LOCOMOTIVE ALLOCATIONS 1948 - 1968

PART TWO :

Southern Region (ex Southern Railway)
Numbers 30001 - 36006, W1 - W36

TRANSPORT PUBLISHING LTD.

First Edition   *December 2006*
Reprinted   *April 2007*
2nd Reprint   *August 2007*
3rd Reprint   *May 2008*

Published by TRANSPORT PUBLISHING LTD,
31 Crown Street, Ayr, KA8 8AG

www.transportpublishing.com

Text printed in Scotland by TRANSPORT PUBLISHING LTD.,
31 Crown Street, Ayr, KA8 8AG

ISBN 13   978 0 9544264 2 2

BRITISH RAILWAYS LOCOMOTIVES 1948 -1968

PART TWO : Southern Region (ex S.R.)
Numbers 30001 - 36006, W1 - W36

Aimed at Railway Enthusiasts, Historians & Modellers, the purpose of this series of books is to list every locomotive acquired and built by British Railways, and to show where they were allocated.

Alongside each locomotive in Part One are the shed allocations for the years 1948, 1952, 1955, 1959, 1963, & 1966

Because of the random, unmethodical, way that Southern Railway locos were numbered, class details are given in Section One. They are then listed in numerical order with allocations & withdrawal dates in Section Two.

JIM GRINDLAY
Ayr, Scotland
November 2006

Introduction to Part Two

What a Railway the Southern was!

Formed in 1923 from the London & South Western, the London, Brighton and South Coast, and the South Eastern and Chatham Railways, the Southern was heavily committed to electrification on a grand scale right from the word go, having inherited the very successful L.S.W.R. 3-rail system, and the L.B.& S.C's overhead electric system, which was later converted to third rail. Therefore, steam took a bit of a 'back seat' when it came to allocating financial resources.

At the grouping there was a very healthy stud of steam locomotives from all three constituents, many of which were fairly modern and fully up to the duties expected from them.

Maunsell, the new group C.M.E. (ex South Eastern & Chatham), added some fine classes with the modified 'King Arthurs', the 'Schools' and the 'Lord Nelsons', along with L1 4-4-0s, N, N1, U & U1 moguls and the Q class 0-6-0s; all good performers after initial teething troubles had been ironed out.

When Maunsell retired, he was replaced by Nigel Gresley's assistant on the L.N.E.R., Oliver V. Bulleid, who raised the eyebrows of the railway fraternity with his bright malachite green livery with sunshine lettering - and then shocked them totally with his air smoothed pacifics, and apoplectic Q1 class 0-6-0s which looked like nothing ever seen before on railways anywhere in the world! But they were brilliant - even if the chain drives encased in baths of oil caused some problems, the 4-6-2s were good locomotives and lasted until the end of steam. The Q1 0-6-0s were power rated 5F by British Railways, but could outperform nominally more powerful locos with ease. A pity about the 'Leader' class - oil firing might have solved some problems, but, in fairness to Bulleid, he was no longer in the saddle when they first appeared and never got the chance to properly develop them.

A very high proportion of pre group ex - Southern locos lasted into the 1960s, because they were solid, dependable workhorses which could be relied upon to do their allotted tasks efficiently and economically. Stroudley's A1x 0-6-0Ts, Drummond's M7s, Maunsell's rebuilt D1s & E1s (later perpetuated in S.R. days as the L1 class for new construction), were all prime examples of pre grouping locomotive engineering at it's best, as were the masterly 'Schools' class and the 'Merchant Navy', and 'West Country / Battle of Britain' classes in Southern days.

In addition, the publicity derived from the names of Southern locomotives was invaluable - who wouldn't turn their head when 'King Arthur' or 'Sir Francis Drake' came into their platform, or get a lump of pride in their throat when 'Spitfire' or 'Fighter Command' or 'Winston Churchill' was at the head of their train. To name these light pacifics after the most famous, and don't forget, a fairly recent victorious air battle, was utterly inspired!

BRITISH RAILWAYS MOTIVE POWER DEPOT CODES
1948 - 1966

In the table below are the Motive Power Depot Codes for the years under review in this publication. There were several changes, both area and regional, made over the years, and the current code for a particular year is shown in the Locomotive Lists. This results in some locomotives which were allocated to the same depot for years on end having two, or even more, different shed codes!

The 1948 column shows the shedcodes in use by the four pre - nationalisation companies; it was not until 1950 that the L.M.S. system was adopted for **all** B.R. sheds. (1949 for Scottish Region).

Under the B.R. System, Shedcodes were allocated as follows:

1 - 29	LONDON MIDLAND REGION	30 - 49	EASTERN REGION
50 - 59	NORTH EASTERN REGION	60 - 69	SCOTTISH REGION
70 - 79	SOUTHERN REGION	80 - 89	WESTERN REGION

Where two companies shared a depot before Nationalisation, the B.R. shedcode is shown against both original codes on two lines, the second line being shown thus "

Sub Sheds & Stabling Points of Main Sheds *are shown in italics.*

Locomotive Shed	1948	1952	1955	1959	1963	1966
Willesden	1A	1A	1A	1A	1A	1A
Camden	1B	1B	1B	1B	1B	1B
Watford	1C	1C	1C	1C	1C	1C
Devons Road (Bow)	13B	1D	1D	1D	1D	1D
Bletchley	2B	1E	1E	1E	1E	1E
Leighton Buzzard	*2B*	*1E*	*1E*	*1E*	-	-
Newport Pagnell	*2B*	*1E*	*1E*	-	-	-
Rugby	2A	2A	2A	2A	2A	1F
Market Harborough	*2A*	*2A*	*2A*	15F	*15C*	*15A*
Seaton	2A	2A	2A	15F	15C	-
Nuneaton	2D	2B	2B	2B	2B	5E
Warwick Milverton	2E	2C	2C	-	-	-
Coventry	2F	2D	2D	2D	-	-
Northampton	2C	2E	2E	2E	2E	1H
Bescot	3A	3A	3A	3A	21B	2F
Bushbury	3B	3B	3B	3B	21C	-
Walsall	3C	3C	3C	3C	21F	2G
Aston	3D	3D	3D	3D	21D	-
Monument Lane	3E	3E	3E	3E	21E	2H
Crewe North	5A	5A	5A	5A	5A	5A
Whitchurch	*5A*	*5A*	*5A*	*5A*	-	-
Crewe South	5B	5B	5B	5B	5B	5B
Crewe Gresty Lane	*CWR*	*5B*	*5B*	*5A*	*5B*	-
Stafford	5C	5C	5C	5C	5C	5C
Coalport	*4A*	*5C*	-	-	-	-
Stoke	5D	5D	5D	5D	5D	5D
Alsager	5E	5E	5E	5E	-	-
Uttoxeter	5F	5F	5F	5F	5F	-
Chester LMS	6A	6A	6A	6A	6A	6A
Mold Junction	6B	6B	6B	6B	6B	6B
Birkenhead LMS Jt	6C	6C	6C	6C	6C	8H
Birkenhead GWR Jt	BHD	"	"	"	"	"
Chester (Northgate)	6D	6D	6D	6D	-	-
Wrexham	6E	6E	6E	6E	-	-
Bidston	6F	6F	6F	6F	6F	-
Llandudno Jnct.	7A	6G	6G	6G	6G	6G
Bangor	7B	6H	6H	6H	6H	-
Holyhead	7C	6J	6J	6J	6J	6J
Rhyl	7D	6K	6K	6K	6K	-
Denbigh	*7D*	*6K*	*6K*	-	-	-

Locomotive Shed	1948	1952	1955	1959	1963	1966
Liverpool Edge Hill	8A	8A	8A	8A	8A	8A
Warrington Dallam	8B	8B	8B	8B	8B	8B
Over and Wharton	*8B*					
Warrington Arpley	*8B*	*8B*	*8B*	*8B*	*8B*	
Speke Junction	8C	8C	8C	8C	8C	8C
Widnes	8D	8D	8D	8D	8D	8D
Widnes C.L.C.	*LIV*	8D	-	-	-	-
Liverpool Brunswick	LIV	8E	8E	27F	-	-
Warrington C.L.C.	*LIV*	*8E*	*8E*	27F	-	-
Allerton	-	-	-	-	-	8J
Longsight	9A	9A	9A	9A	9A	9A
Stockport Edgeley	9B	9B	9B	9B	9B	9B
Macclesfield	9C	9C	9C	9C	9C	-
Buxton	9D	9D	9D	9D	9D	9L
Trafford Park LMS	19G	9E	9E	9E	9E	9E
Trafford Park LNER	TFD	"	"	"	"	"
Heaton Mersey LMS	19D	9F	9F	9F	9F	9F
Heaton Mersey LNER	STP	"	"	"	"	"
Northwich	NTH	9G	9G	9G	8E	8E
Springs Branch	10A	10A	10A	8F	8F	8F
Preston	10B	10B	10B	24K	-	-
Patricroft	10C	10C	10C	26F	26F	9H
Bolton Plodder Lane	10D	10D	-	-	-	-
Sutton Oak	10E	10E	10E	8G	8G	8G
Carnforth	11A	11A	11A	24L	24L	10A
Barrow	11B	11B	11B	11A	12E	12C
Lakeside	*11B*	-	-	-	-	-
Coniston	*11B*	*11B*	*11B*	-	-	-
Oxenholme	11C	11C	11C	11C	-	-
Tebay	11D	11D	*11D*	11D	12H	12E
Lancaster Green Ayre	20H	11E	11E	24J	24J	10J
Carlisle Kingmoor	12A	68A	68A	12A	12A	12A
Carlisle Upperby	12B	12A	12A	12B	12B	12B
Carlisle Canal	CAR	68E	68E	12C	12C	-
Penrith	12C	12C	12C	*12B*	-	-
Workington	12D	12D	12D	11B	12F	12D
Moor Row	12E	12E	-	-	-	-

Locomotive Shed	1948	1952	1955	1959	1963	1966
Cricklewood	14A	14A	14A	14A	14A	-
Cricklewood East	-	-	-	-	-	14A
Cricklewood West	-	-	-	-	-	14B
Kentish Town	14B	14B	14B	14B	14B	-
St. Albans	14C	14C	14C	14C	-	-
Marylebone	-	-	-	-	14F	1D
Wellingborough	15A	15A	15A	15A	15A	15B
Kettering	15B	15B	15B	15B	15B	-
Leicester (Midland)	15C	15C	15C	15C	15C	15A
Bedford	15D	15D	15D	14E	14E	14C
Nottingham	16A	16A	16A	16A	16A	16D
Southwell	16A	16A	16A	-	-	-
Lincoln (Midland)	16A	16A	-	-	-	-
Kirkby	16C	16C	16C	16B	16B	16E
Mansfield	16D	16D	16D	16C	-	-
Derby	17A	17A	17A	17A	17A	16C
Burton	17B	17B	17B	17B	17B	16F
Overseal	17B	17B	17B	17B	17B	16F
Coalville	17C	17C	17C	15D	15D	15E
Rowsley	17D	17D	17D	17D	17C	-
Cromford	9D	17D	17D	17D	17C	16C
Middleton	9D	17D	17D	17D	17C	9L
Sheep Pasture	9D	17D	17D	17D	17C	16C
Toton	18A	18A	18A	18A	18A	16A
Westhouses	18B	18B	18B	18B	18B	16G
Hasland	18C	18C	18C	18C	18C	-
Clay Cross	18C	18C	18C	-	-	-
Staveley	18D	18D	18D	41E	41E	41E
Sheepbridge	18D	18D	18D	-	-	-
Grimesthorpe	19A	19A	19A	41B	-	-
Millhouses	19B	19B	19B	41C	-	-
Canklow	19C	19C	19C	41D	41D	41D
Leeds Holbeck	20A	20A	20A	55A	55A	55A
Stourton	20B	20B	20B	55B	55B	55B
Royston	20C	20C	20C	55D	55D	55D
Normanton	20D	20D	20D	55E	55E	55E
Manningham	20E	20E	20E	55F	55F	55F
Ilkley	20E	20E	20E	55A	52G	-
Ilkley (ex LNER)	ILK	20E	20E	-	-	-
Skipton	20F	20F	20F	24G	24G	10G
Keighley	20F	20F	20F	55F	55F	55F
Ingleton	20F	20G	20G	-	-	-
Hellifield	20G	20G	20G	24H	24H	-
Saltley	21A	21A	21A	21A	21A	2E
Bournville	21B	21B	21B	21B	-	
Redditch	21B	21B	21B	85F	85D	85D
Bromsgrove	21C	21C	21C	85F	85D	85D
Stratford-on-Avon LMS	21D	21D	21A	-	-	-
Bristol Barrow Road	22A	22A	22A	82E	82E	-
Gloucester Barnwood	22B	22B	22B	85E	85C	-
Tewkesbury	22B	22B	22B	85E	-	-
Dursley	22B	22B	22B	85E	-	-
Accrington	24A	24A	24A	24A	24A	10E
Rose Grove	24B	24B	24B	24B	24B	10F
Lostock Hall	24C	24C	24C	24C	24C	10D
Lower Darwen	24D	24D	24D	24D	24D	-
Blackpool	24E	24E	24E	24E	24E	10B
Blackpool North	24E	24E	24E	-	-	-
Fleetwood	24F	24F	24F	24F	24F	-

Locomotive Shed	1948	1952	1955	1959	1963	1966
Wakefield	25A	25A	25A	56A	56A	56A
Huddersfield	25B	25B	25B	55G	55G	55G
Goole	25C	25C	25C	53E	50D	50D
Mirfield	25D	25D	25D	56D	56D	56D
Sowerby Bridge	25E	25E	25E	56E	56E	-
Low Moor	25F	25F	25F	56F	56F	56F
Farnley Junction	25G	25G	25G	55C	55C	55C
Newton Heath	26A	26A	26A	26A	26A	9D
Agecroft	26B	26B	26B	26B	26B	9J
Bolton	26C	26C	26C	26C	26C	9K
Bury	26D	26D	26D	26D	26D	-
Bacup	26E	26E	26E	-	-	-
Lees	26F	26F	26F	26E	26E	-
Belle Vue	19E	26G	26G	-	-	-
Bank Hall	23A	27A	27A	27A	27A	8K
Aintree	23B	27B	27B	27B	27B	8L
Southport	23C	27C	27C	27C	27C	-
Wigan (L& Y)	23D	27D	27D	27D	27D	-
Walton-on-the-Hill	WAL	27E	27E	27E	27E	-
Southport (C.L.C.)	LIV	27E	-	-	-	-
Stratford	STR	30A	30A	30A	30A	30A
Brentwood	STR	30A	30A	-	-	-
Chelmsford	STR	30A	30A	30A	-	-
Epping	STR	30A	30A	-	-	-
Spitalfields	STR	30A	-	-	-	-
Walthamstow	STR	30A	30A	-	-	-
Palace Gates	STR	30A	30A	-	-	-
Enfield Town	STR	30A	30A	30A	-	-
Ware	STR	30A	30A	-	-	-
Hertford East	STR	30B	30B	30B	-	-
Buntingford	STR	30B	30B	30B	-	-
Bishops Stortford	STR	30C	30C	30C	-	-
Southend Victoria	STR	30D	30D	30A	-	-
Southminster	STR	30D	30D	-	-	-
Wickford	STR	30D	-	-	-	-
Colchester	COL	30E	30E	30E	-	-
Clacton	COL	30E	30E	30E	-	-
Walton-on-Naze	COL	30E	30E	30E	-	-
Kelvedon	COL	30E	30E	-	-	-
Maldon	COL	30E	30E	30E	-	-
Braintree	COL	30E	30E	30E	-	-
Parkeston	PKS	30F	30F	30F	30F	30F
Cambridge	CAM	31A	31A	31A	31A	31A
Ely	CAM	31A	31A	31A	31A	31A
Huntingdon East	CAM	31A	31A	31A	-	-
Saffron Walden	CAM	31A	31A	31A	-	-
Thaxted	CAM	31A	31A			
March	MAR	31B	31B	31B	31B	31B
Kings Lynn	KL	31C	31C	31C	-	-
Wisbech	KL	31C	31C	31B	-	-
Hunstanton	KL	31C	31C	31C	-	-
South Lynn	SL	31D	31D	31D	-	-
Bury St. Edmunds	BSE	31E	31E	31E	-	-
Sudbury	BSE	31E	31E	31E	-	-
Norwich	NOR	32A	32A	32A	32A	32A
Cromer	NOR	32A	32A	32A	32A	32A
Wells-on-Sea	NOR	32A	32A	-	-	-
Dereham	NOR	32A	32A	32A	-	-
Swaffham	NOR	32A	32A	-	-	-
Wymondham	NOR	32A	32A	32A	-	-
Ipswich	IPS	32B	32B	32B	32B	32B

Locomotive Shed	1948	1952	1955	1959	1963	1966
Ipswich	IPS	32B	32B	32B	32B	32B
Laxfield	IPS	32B	-	-	-	-
Felixstowe Beach	IPS	32B	32B	32B	-	-
Aldeburgh	IPS	32B	32B	-	-	-
Framlingham	IPS	32B	-	-	-	-
Stowmarket	IPS	32B	32B	32B	-	-
Lowestoft	LOW	32C	32C	32C	32C	32C
Yarmouth (South Town)	YAR	32D	32D	32D	32D	32D
Yarmouth (Vauxhall)	YAR	32E	32E	32E	-	-
Yarmouth (Beach)	YB	32F	32F	-	-	-
Melton Constable	MC	32G	32G	32G	-	-
Norwich City	MC	32G	32G	32G	-	-
Cromer Beach	MC	32G	32G	-	-	-
Plaistow	13A	33A	33A	33A	-	-
Upminster	13E	33A	33A	-	-	-
Tilbury	13C	33B	33B	33B	33B	-
Shoeburyness	13D	33C	33C	33C	33C	-
Kings Cross	KX	34A	34A	34A	34A	-
Hornsey	HSY	34B	34B	34B	34B	34B
Hatfield	HAT	34C	34C	34C	-	-
Hitchin	HIT	34D	34D	34D	34D	34D
Neasden	NEA	34E	34E	14D	14F	-
Aylesbury	NEA	34E	34E	14D	-	-
Chesham	NEA	34E	34E	14D	-	-
Finsbury Park	-	-	-	-	34G	34G
New England	NWE	35A	35A	34E	34E	34E
Spalding	NWE	35A	35A	-	-	-
Bourne	NWE	35A	35A	-	-	-
Stamford	NWE	35A	35A	-	-	-
Grantham	GRA	35B	35B	34F	34F	-
Peterborough Spital	16B	35C	35C	31F	-	-
Doncaster	DON	36A	36A	36A	36A	36A
Mexborough	MEX	36B	36B	41F	41F	-
Frodingham	FRO	36C	36C	36C	36C	36C
Barnsley	BRN	36D	36D	-	-	-
Retford	RET	36E	36E	36E	36E	-
Newark	GRA	36E	36E	36E	-	-
Ardsley	ARD	37A	37A	56B	56B	56B
Copley Hill	COP	37B	37B	56C	56C	-
Bradford	BFD	37C	37C	56G	56G	56G
Colwick	CLK	38A	38A	40E	40E	16B
Derby Friargate	CLK	38A	38A	17A	-	-
Annesley	ANN	38B	38B	16D	16D	-
Leicester (ex G.C.)	LEI	38C	38C	15E	15E	-
Leicester (ex G.N.)	LEI	38C	38C	-	-	-
Staveley (Ex G.C.)	STV	38D	38D	41H	41H	-
Woodford Halse	WFD	38E	38E	-	-	-
Gorton	GOR	39A	39A	9G	9G	-
Dinting	GOR	39A	39A	9G	9G	-
Hayfield	GOR	39A	39A	-	-	-
Macclesfield	GOR	39A	39A	9C	-	-
Sheffield Darnall	SHF	39B	39B	41A	41A	-
Lincoln	LIN	40A	40A	40A	40A	40A
Immingham	IMM	40B	40B	40B	40B	40B
Louth	LTH	40C	40C	-	-	-
Tuxford	TUX	40D	40D	41K	-	-
Langwith Junction	LNG	40E	40E	41J	41J	41J
Boston	BOS	40F	40F	40F	40F	40F

Locomotive Shed	1948	1952	1955	1959	1963	1966
Sheffield Tinsley	-	-	-	-	-	41A
Shirebrook West	-	-	-	-	-	41A
York	YK	50A	50A	50A	50A	50A
Leeds (Neville Hill)	NEV	50B	50B	50B	55H	55H
Selby	SEL	50C	50C	50C	-	-
Starbeck	SBK	50D	50D	50D	-	-
Scarborough	SCA	50E	50E	50E	50E	-
Malton	MAL	50F	50F	50F	50F	-
Pickering	MAL	50F	50F	50F	-	-
Whitby	WBY	50G	50G	50G	-	-
Darlington	DAR	51A	51A	51A	51A	51A
Middleton-in-Teesdale	DAR	51A	51A	51A	-	-
Newport	NPT	51B	51B	-	-	-
West Hartlepool	WHL	51C	51C	51C	51C	51C
Middlesbrough	MID	51D	51D	-	-	-
Guisborough	MID	51D	51D	-	-	-
Stockton	SKN	51E	51E	51E	-	-
West Aukland	AUK	51F	51F	51F	51F	-
Wearhead	AUK	51F	51F	-	-	-
Haverton Hill	HAV	51G	51G	51G	-	-
Kirkby Stephen	KBY	51H	51H	-	-	-
Northallerton	NLN	51J	51J	51J	51J	-
Leyburn	NLN	51J	51J	-	-	-
Saltburn	SAL	51K	51K	-	-	-
Thornaby	-	-	-	51L	51L	51L
Gateshead	GHD	52A	52A	52A	52A	52A
Bowes Bridge	GHD	52A	52A	52A	52A	52A
Heaton	HTN	52B	52B	52B	52B	52B
Blaydon	BLA	52C	52C	52C	52C	52C
Hexham	BLA	52C	52C	52C	-	-
Alston	BLA	52C	52C	52C	52C	52C
Reedsmouth	BLA	52C	52C	-	-	-
Tweedmouth	TWD	52D	52D	52D	52D	52D
Alnmouth	TWD	52D	52D	52D	52D	52D
Percy Main	PMN	52E	52E	52E	52E	52E
North Blyth	NBH	52F	52F	52F	52F	52F
South Blyth	NBH	52F	52F	52F	52F	52F
Rothbury	NBH	52F	52F	-	-	-
Hull (Dairycotes)	HLD	53A	53A	53A	50B	50B
Hull (Botanic Gardens)	HLB	53B	53B	53B	50C	50C
Hull (Springhead)	HLS	53C	53C	53C	-	-
Alexandra Dock	HLS	53C	53C	53C	50B	-
Bridlington	BRI	53D	53D	53D	-	-
Sunderland	SUN	54A	54A	52G	52G	52G
Durham	SUN	54A	54A	52G	-	-
Tyne Dock	TDK	54B	54B	52H	52H	52H
Pelton Level	TDK	54B	54B	52H	52H	-
Borough Gardens	BOR	54C	54C	52J	-	-
Consett	CON	54D	54D	52K	52K	52K
Inverness	32A	60A	60A	60A	60A	60A
Dingwall	32A	60A	60A	60A	60A	-
Fortrose	32A	60A	60A	-	-	-
Kyle of Lochalsh	32A	60A	60A	60A	60A	60A
Aviemore	32B	60B	60B	60B	60B	60B
Boat of Garten	KEI	60B	60B	60B	60B	-
Helmsdale	32A	60C	60C	60C	60C	-
Dornoch	32A	60C	60C	-	-	-
Tain	32A	60C	60C	60C	60C	-
Wick	32A	60D	60D	60D	60D	60D
Thurso	32A	60D	60D	60D	60D	60D
Forres	32C	60E	60E	60E	60A	60A

Locomotive Shed	1948	1952	1955	1959	1963	1966
Kittybrewster	KIT	61A	61A	61A	61A	61A
Ballater	KIT	61A	61A	61A	61A	61A
Fraserburgh	KIT	61A	61A	61A	61A	61A
Peterhead	KIT	61A	61A	61A	61A	61A
Inverurie	-	-	-	61A	61A	61A
Ferryhill L.M.S	29B	61B	61B	61B	61B	61B
Ferryhill L.N.E.R	ABD	"	"	"	"	"
Keith	KEI	61C	61C	61C	61C	61C
Banff	KEI	61C	61C	61C	61C	-
Elgin	KEI	61C	61C	61C	61C	61C
Thornton Jnct.	THJ	62A	62A	62A	62A	62A
Anstruther	THJ	62A	62A	62A	62A	62A
Burntisland	THJ	62A	62A	62A	62A	62A
Ladybank	THJ	62A	62A	62A	62A	62A
Methil	THJ	62A	62A	62A	62A	62A
Kirkcaldy	-	-	-	62A	62A	62A
Dundee	DEE	62B	62B	62B	62B	62B
Dundee West	29C	62B	62B	62B	-	-
Arbroath	29D	62B	62B	62B	62B	-
Montrose	DEE	62B	62B	62B	62B	62B
St. Andrews	DEE	62B	62B	62B	62B	62B
Dunfermline Upper	DFU	62C	62C	62C	62C	62C
Alloa	STG	62C	62C	62C	62C	62C
Kelty	DFU	62C	62C	62C	62C	-
Perth LMS	29A	63A	63A	63A	63A	63A
Perth LNER	PTH	63A	63A	63A	63A	63A
Aberfeldy	29A	63A	63A	63A	63A	63A
Blair Atholl	29A	63A	63A	63A	63A	63A
Crieff	29A	63A	63A	63A	63A	63A
Stirling	31B	63B	63B	63B	65J	65J
Killin	29D	63B	63B	63B	65J	-
Stirling Shore Road	STG	63B	63B	-	-	-
Forfar	29D	63C	63C	63C	63A	-
Brechin	29D	63C	63C	-	-	-
Fort William	FW	63D	63D	65J	63B	63B
Mallaig	FW	63D	63D	65J	63B	63B
Oban	31C	63E	63E	63D	63C	63C
Ballachulish	31C	63E	63E	63D	63C	63C
St. Margarets	STM	64A	64A	64A	64A	64A
Dunbar	STM	64A	64A	64A	64A	-
Galashiels	STM	64A	64A	64A	64A	64A
Granton	-	-	-	-	64A	64A
Hardengreen	STM	64A	64A	64A	64A	-
Longniddry	STM	64A	64A	64A	64A	-
North Berwick	STM	64A	64A	64A	64A	64A
Peebles	STM	64A	64A	-	-	-
Seafield	STM	64A	64A	64A	64A	-
South Leith	-	-	-	64A	64A	64A
Haymarket	HAY	64B	64B	64B	64B	64B
Dalry Road	28B	64C	64C	64C	64C	64C
Carstairs	28C	64D	64D	64D	66E	66E
Polmont	POL	64E	64E	64E	65K	-
Bathgate	BGT	64F	64F	64F	64F	64F
Hawick	HAW	64G	64G	64G	64G	64G
Kelso	HAW	64G	64G	-	-	-
Riccarton	HAW	64G	64G	64G	-	-
St. Boswells	HAW	64G	64G	64G	-	-
Leith Central	-	-	-	64H	64H	64H
Eastfield	EFD	65A	65A	65A	65A	65A
St. Rollox	31A	65B	65B	65B	65B	65B
Parkhead	PKD	65C	65C	65C	65C	-
Dawsholm	31E	65D	65D	65D	65D	-

Locomotive Shed	1948	1952	1955	1959	1963	1966
Dumbarton	31E	65D	65D	65D	65D	65D
Kipps	KPS	65E	65E	65E	65E	65E
Grangemouth	31D	65F	65F	65F	65F	65F
Yoker	31E	65G	65G	65G	65G	-
Helensburgh	PKD	65H	65H	65H	65H	-
Arrochar	EFD	65H	65H	65A	65A	-
Balloch	EFD	65I	65I	65I	65I	-
Polmadie	27A	66A	66A	66A	66A	66A
Motherwell	28A	66B	66B	66B	66B	66B
Morningside	BGT	66B	-	-	-	-
Hamilton	27C	66C	66C	66C	66C	66C
Greenock Ladyburn	27B	66D	66D	66D	66D	66D
Greenock Princes Pier	27B	66D	66D	-	-	-
Corkerhill	30A	67A	67A	67A	67A	67A
Hurlford	30B	67B	67B	67B	67B	67B
Beith	30B	67B	67B	67B	67B	-
Muirkirk	30B	67B	67B	67B	67B	-
Ayr	30D	67C	67C	67C	67C	67C
Ardrossan	30C	67D	67D	67D	67D	-
Carlisle Kingmoor	12A	68A	68A	12A	12A	12A
Dumfries	12G	68B	68B	68B	67E	67E
Kircudbright	12G	68B	68B	-	-	-
Stranraer	12H	68C	68C	68C	67F	67F
Newton Stewart	12H	68C	68C	68C	-	-
Beattock	12F	68D	68D	68D	66F	66F
Carlisle Canal	CAR	68E	68E	12C	-	-
Nine Elms	9E	70A	70A	70A	70A	70A
Feltham	FEL	70B	70B	70B	70B	70B
Guildford	GFD	70C	70C	70C	70C	70C
Bordon	GFD	70C	-	-	-	-
Basingstoke	BAS	70D	70D	70D	70D	70D
Reading	RDG	70E	70E	70E	70C	70C
Eastleigh	ELH	71A	71A	71A	71A	70D
Winchester (SR)	ELH	71A	71A	71A	71A	-
Winchester (WR)	WIN	71A	71A	-	-	-
Lymington	LYM	71A	71A	71A	-	-
Andover Junction	AND	71A	71A	71A	71A	-
Bournemouth	BM	71B	71B	71B	71B	70F
Swanage	BM	71B	71B	-	-	-
Hamworthy Jnct.	BM	71B	-	-	-	-
Branksome	22C	71B	71B	71B	71B	70F
Dorchester	DOR	71C	71C	71B	71B	-
Fratton	FRA	71D	70F	70F	-	-
Gosport	FRA	71D	-	-	-	-
Midhurst	FRA	71D	-	-	-	-
Newport (I.O.W.)	NPT	71E	70G	-	-	-
Ryde (I.O.W.)	RYD	71F	70H	70H	70H	70H
Bath (S. & D.)	22C	71G	71G	82F	82F	82F
Radstock	22C	71G	71G	82F	82F	82F
Templecombe	22D	71H	71H	82G	82G	83G
Southampton Docks	SOT	71I	71I	71I	71I	70I
Highbridge	22E	71J	71J	82F	82F	82F
Exmouth Jnct.	EXJ	72A	72A	72A	72A	83D
Seaton	EXJ	72A	72A	72A	72A	-
Lyme Regis	EXJ	72A	72A	72A	72A	-
Exmouth	EXJ	72A	72A	72A	72A	-
Okehampton	EXJ	72A	72A	72A	72A	83D
Bude	EXJ	72A	72A	72A	72A	83D
Salisbury	SAL	72B	72B	72B	70E	70E

Locomotive Shed	1948	1952	1955	1959	1963	1966
Yeovil Town	YEO	72C	72C	72C	72C	83E
Plymouth	PLY	72D	72D	83H	83H	-
Callington	PLY	72D	72D	72A	72A	-
Barnstaple Jnct.	BPL	72E	72E	72E	72E	-
Torrington	BPL	72E	72E	72E	-	-
Ilfracombe	BPL	72E	72E	72E	72E	-
Wadebridge	WAD	72F	72F	72F	72F	84E
Stewarts Lane	BAT	73A	73A	73A	75D	75D
Bricklayers Arms	BA	73B	73B	73B	-	-
Hither Green	HIT	73C	73C	73C	73C	73C
Gillingham (Kent)	GIL	73D	73D	73D	-	-
Faversham	FAV	73E	73E	73E	73D	-
Ashford (Kent)	AFD	74A	74A	73F	73F	73F
Canterbury West	AFD	74A	74A	-	-	-
Ramsgate	RAM	74B	74B	73G	-	-
Dover	DOV	74C	74C	73H	-	-
Folkestone Jnct.	DOV	74C	74C	73H	-	-
Tonbridge	TON	74D	74D	73J	-	-
St. Leonards	STL	74E	74E	73D	73D	73D
Brighton	BTN	75A	75A	75A	75A	75A
Newhaven	BTN	75A	75A	75A	-	-
Redhill	RED	75B	75B	75B	75B	-
Norwood Junction	NOR	75C	75C	75C	75C	-
Selhurst	-	-	-	-	-	75C
Horsham	HOR	75D	75D	75D	75E	-
Three Bridges	3B	75E	75E	75E	75E	-
Tunbridge Wells West	TWW	75F	75F	75F	75F	-
Eastbourne	EBN	75G	-	-	-	-
Old Oak Common	PDN	81A	81A	81A	81A	81A
Slough	SLO	81B	81B	81B	81B	-
Aylesbury	SLO	81B	-	-	-	-
Marlow	SLO	81B	81B	81B	-	-
Watlington	SLO	81B	81B	-	-	-
Southall	SHL	81C	81C	81C	81C	81C
Staines	SHL	81C	-	-	-	-
Reading	RDG	81D	81D	81D	81D	81D
Henley-on-Thames	RDG	81D	81D	81D	-	-
Didcot	DID	81E	81E	81E	81E	81E
Newbury	DID	81E	-	-	-	-
Wallingford	DID	81E	81E	-	-	-
Oxford	OXF	81F	81F	81F	81F	81F
Abingdon	OXF	81F	-	-	-	-
Fairford	OXF	81F	81F	81F	-	-
Bristol Bath Road	BRD	82A	82A	82A	82A	82A
Bath	BRD	82A	82A	82A	-	-
Wells	BRD	82A	82A	82A	-	-
Weston-super-Mare	BRD	82A	82A	82A	-	-
Yatton	BRD	82A	82A	82A	-	-
St. Philip's Marsh	SPM	82B	82B	82B	82B	-
Swindon	SDN	82C	82C	82C	82C	-
Andover Junction	SDN	82C	82C	82C	-	-
Chippenham	SDN	82C	82C	82C	82C	-
Westbury	WES	82D	82D	82D	82D	-
Salisbury	SAL	-	-	-	-	-
Frome	WES	82D	82D	82D	-	-
Yeovil Pen Mill	YEO	82E	82E	71H	-	-
Weymouth	WEY	82F	82F	71G	71G	70G
Bridport	WEY	82F	82F	71G	-	-
Newton Abbot	NA	83A	83A	83A	83A	83A

Locomotive Shed	1948	1952	1955	1959	1963	1966
Ashburton	NA	83A	83A	-	-	-
Kingsbridge	NA	83A	83A	83A	-	-
Taunton	TN	83B	83B	83B	83B	83B
Bridgwater	TN	83B	83B	83B	-	-
Minehead	TN	83B	83B	-	-	-
Exeter	EXE	83C	83C	83C	83C	-
Tiverton Junction	EXE	83C	83C	83C	83C	-
Plymouth Laira	LA	83D	83D	83D	83D	84A
Princetown	LA	83D	83D	-	-	-
Launceston	LA	83D	83D	83D	83D	-
St. Blazey	SBZ	83E	83E	83E	83E	84B
Bodmin	SBZ	83E	83E	83E	-	-
Moorswater	SBZ	83E	83E	83E	-	-
Truro	TR	83F	83F	83F	83F	84C
Penzance	PZ	83G	83G	83G	83G	84D
Helston	PZ	83G	83G	83G	-	-
St. Ives	PZ	83G	83G	83G	-	-
Wolverhampton	SRD	84A	84A	84A	84A	-
Oxley	OXY	84B	84B	84B	84B	2B
Banbury	BAN	84C	84C	84C	84C	2D
Leamington Spa	LMTN	84D	84D	84D	84D	-
Tyseley	TYS	84E	84E	84E	84E	2A
Stratford-on-Avon	21D	84E	84E	84E	84E	2A
Stourbridge	STB	84F	84F	84F	84F	-
Shrewsbury LMS	4A	84G	84G	84G	89A	6D
Shrewsbury GW	SALOP	"	"	"	"	"
Clee Hill	4A	84G	84G	84G		-
Cravens Arms	4A	84G	84G	84G	86C	-
Knighton	4A	84G	84G	84G		
Builth Road	4A	84G	84G	84G	89A	6D
Wellington	WLN	84H	84H	84H	84H	-
Croes Newydd	CNYD	84J	84J	84J	89B	6C
Bala	CNYD	84J	84J	84J	89B	-
Trawsfynydd	CNYD	84J	84J	84J	-	-
Penmaenpool	CNYD	84J	84J	84J	89B	-
Chester G.W.R.	CHR	84K	84K	6E	-	-
Worcester	WOS	85A	85A	85A	85A	85A
Honeybourne	-	-	-	-	85A	85A
Evesham	WOS	85A	85A	85A	-	-
Kingham	WOS	85A	85A	85A	-	-
Gloucester	GLO	85B	85B	85B	85B	85B
Cheltenham	CHEL	85B	85B	85B	85B	-
Brimscombe	CHEL	85B	85B	85B	85B	-
Cirencester	CHEL	85B	85B	85B	-	-
Lydney	LYD	85B	85B	85B	85B	-
Tetbury	LYD	85B	85B	85B	-	-
Hereford	HFD	85C	85C	85C	86C	-
Leominster	HFD	85C	85C	85C	-	-
Ross	HFD	85C	85C	85C	-	-
Kidderminster	KDR	85D	85D	85D	84G	-
Ebbw Junction	NPT	86A	86A	86A	86A	86B
Newport Pill	PILL	86B	86B	86B	86B	-
Cardiff (Canton)	CDF	86C	86C	86C	88A	86A
Llantrisant	LTS	86D	86D	86D	88G	-
Severn Tunnel Jnct.	STJ	86E	86E	86E	86E	86E
Tondu	TDU	86F	86F	86F	88H	-
Pontypool Road	PPRD	86G	86G	86G	86G	-
Branches Fork	PPRD	86G	-	-	-	-
Aberbeeg	ABEEG	86H	86H	86H	86F	-
Aberdare	ABDR	86J	86J	86J	88J	-
Abergavenny	4D	86K	86K	-	-	-
Tredegar	4E	86K	86K	86K	-	-

A smart looking Class 'M7' 0-4-4T, No. 30319, which was withdrawn from Nine Elms during January 1960. The 'M7's were a very competent Drummond design for the London & South Western Railway, and most of them had a lifespan of around sixty years.

Locomotive Shed	1948	1952	1955	1959	1963	1966
Neath	NEA	87A	87A	87A	87A	87A
Margam	-	-	-	-	-	87B
Glyn Neath	NEA	87A	87A	87A	87A	-
Neath (N. & B.)	NEA	87A	87A	87A	87A	-
Duffryn Yard	DYD	87B	87B	87B	87B	-
Danygraig	DG	87C	87C	87C	87C	-
Swansea East Dock	SED	87D	87D	87D	87D	87E
Landore	LDR	87E	87E	87E	87E	87F
Llanelly	LLY	87F	87F	87F	87F	-
Burry Port	LLY	87F	87F	87F	-	-
Pantyfynnon	LLY	87F	87F	87F	87F	-
Carmarthen	CARM	87G	87G	87G	87G	-
Newcastle Emlyn	CARM	87G	-	-	-	-
Neyland	NEY	87H	87H	87H	87H	-
Cardigan	WTD	87H	87H	87H	-	-
Milford Haven	NEY	87H	87H	87H	-	-
Pembroke Dock	WTD	87H	87H	87H	87H	87H
Whitland	WTD	87H	87H	87H	87H	-
Goodwick	FGD	87J	87J	87J	87J	-
Swansea Victoria	4B	87K	87K	87K	-	-
Llandovery	4B	87K	87K	87K	87F	-
Upper Bank	4C	87K	87K	87K	-	-
Gurnos	4C	87K	87K	87K	-	-
Cardiff Cathays	CHYS	88A	88A	88A	88M	-
Radyr	RYR	88A	88A	88A	88B	-
Cardiff East Dock	CED	88B	88B	88B	88L	-
Barry	BRY	88C	88C	88C	88C	-
Merthyr	MTHR	88D	88D	88D	88D	-
Cae Harris	CH	88D	88D	88D	88D	-
Dowlais Central	DLS	88D	88D	88D	88D	-
Rhymney	RHY	88D	88D	88D	88D	-
Abercynon	AYN	88E	88E	88E	88E	-
Treherbert	THT	88F	88F	88F	88F	-
Ferndale	FDL	88F	88F	88F	88F	-

Locomotive Shed	1948	1952	1955	1959	1963	1.
Oswestry	OSW	89A	89A	89A	89D	-
Llanfyllin	OSW	89A	-	-	-	-
Llanidloes	OSW	89A	89A	89A	89D	-
Moat Lane	OSW	89A	89A	89A	89D	-
Welshpool (W & L)	OSW	89A	89A	-	-	-
Brecon	BCN	89B	89B	89B	-	-
Builth Wells	BCN	89B	89B	-	-	-
Machynlleth	MCH	89C	89C	89C	89C	6F
Aberayron	MCH	89C	89C	89C	-	-
Aberystwyth	ABH	89C	89C	89C	89C	-
Aberystwyth (V of R)	-	-	-	89C	89C	6F
Portmadoc	MCH	89C	89C	89C	89C	6F
Pwllheli	MCH	89C	89C	89C	89C	6F
Western A.C. Lines					ACL	ACL
Western Lines						WL
Midland Lines						ML
London (W) Division						D01
Birmingham Division						D02
Stoke Division						D03
London (M) Division						D14
Leicester Division						D15
Nottingham Division						D16
Crewe Works	CW	CW	CW	CW	CW	CW
Derby Works	DW	DW	DW	DW	DW	DW
Horwich Works	HW	HW	HW	HW	HW	HW
Wolverton Works	WW	WW	WW	WW	WW	WW
St Rollox Works	SRW	SRW	SRW	SRW	SRW	SRW
C.M.E., Crewe		CMEC	CMEC	CMEC	CMEC	CMEC
Rugby Testing Stn.		RTS	RTS	RTS	RTS	RTS

Notes on Using this Book :

1) Locomotives which carried their allocated B. R. Number are shown in bold type :- **67890**. Locomotives which *never* carried their allocated B. R. Number are shown in italics :- *67890*.

2) The building or acquisition date of locos in to stock after 1/1/48, is shown in the '1948' locoshed column in bold italics :- *06/51*

3) *Final* withdrawal dates are also shown in bold italics :- *09/65*

4) Allocation dates shown in this book are as follows:- January 1st 1948, August 1st 1952, January 1st 1955, January 1st 1959, March 1st 1963 and January 1st 1966.

Publishers Note :

Every effort has been made to be 100% accurate, but if there are mistakes, then please let us know, so that we can get them altered for our next print run.

During the research which has gone in to these publications, the writer has obtained information from many different sources including British Railways, the Public Records Office at Kew, the National Library of Scotland, the British Library, the National Railway Museum, the Railway Correspondence and Travel Society, the Stephenson Locomotive Society, and countless professional railwaymen and enthusiasts throughout the length and breadth of the country.

However, the story is not complete. We would like details of all the locomotives which survived into British Railways and never *became* B.R. capital stock, but were used for other duties such as internal shunters, stationery boilers, C.M.E. test locos (like **10897** at Uttoxeter, for instance), generators, either mobile of fixed, etc.. If you have any further information, please email us at

modelmasterbooks@aol.com, or write to :

MODELMASTER PUBLISHING, P.O. Box 8560, TROON, SCOTLAND, KA10 6WX

Class B4 0-4-0T No. 30089 has obviously received special attention from the shed graffiti artist!
Formerly named Trouville, it lasted at Guildford shed until March 1963.

One of Maunsell's big shunters, 'Z' Class 0-8-0T No 30950, takes a break from her duties. All of this class were withdrawn during late 1962. They were pleasing looking locos, with sloping, short, side tanks and an uneven wheelbase.

'Merchant Navy'　　　　Bulleid S.R.　　　　4-6-2

Introduced 1941 by O.V.S. Bulleid. Air smoothed casing, high pressure boiler and chain valve gear. Rebuilt with multiple-jet blastpipe, wide chimney and Walschaerts valve gear. The air smoothed boiler casing was also removed.

Loco Weight : 94t 15c *Driving Wheels :* 6' 2" *Cylinders :* (3) 18" x 24" *Valve Gear :* Bulleid (Piston Valves)

Details when rebuilt:

Loco Weight : 97t 18c *Driving Wheels :* 6' 2" *Cylinders :* (3) 18" x 24" *Valve Gear :* Walschaerts (Piston Valves)

Number Series

35001 - 35030 (formerly S.R. 21C001 - 21C030)　　　　　　　***Total 30***

'West Country' / 'Battle of Britain'　　Bulleid S.R.　　　4-6-2

Introduced 1945 ('West Country' Class for Western Section), and 1946 ('Battle of Britain' Class for Eastern Section), this was a lightweight development of Bulleid's 'Merchant Navy' Class.

Loco Weight : 86t 0c *Driving Wheels :* 6' 2" *Cylinders :* (3) 16⅜" x 24" *Valve Gear :* Bulleid (Piston Valves)

Introduced 1957. Sixty out of the one hundred and ten locos were rebuilt with multiple-jet blastpipe, wide chimney and Walschaerts valve gear. The air smoothed boiler casing was also removed.

Loco Weight : 90t 1c *Driving Wheels :* 6' 2" *Cylinders :* (3) 16⅜" x 24" *Valve Gear :* Walschaerts (Piston Valves)

Number Series

34001 - 34110 (34001 - 34070 formerly S.R. 21C101 - 21C170),　rest built new in B.R. days.

Total 110

LN 'Lord Nelson'　　　　Maunsell S.R.　　　　4-6-0

Built between 1926 - 1929, these four cylinder 4-6-0s were later fitted with smoke deflectors, double blast pipes, and wide chimneys. 30859 had 6' 3" Driving Wheels instead of the usual 6' 7", and 30860 had a longer boiler. 30865 had the crank setting adjusted to give 4 exhausts per revolution instead of the 8 exhausts per revolution of the rest of the class. 30859 weighed 83t 10c.

Loco Weight : 84t 16c *Driving Wheels :* 6' 7" *Cylinders :* (4) 16½" x 26" *Valve Gear :* Walschaerts (Piston Valves)

Number Series

30850 - 30865

Total 16

N15 'King Arthur'　　　L.S.W.R. Urie / Maunsell　　　4-6-0

Built between 1918 and 1926, these 74 locomotives were the backbone of Southern Railway main line steam power until the introduction of Bulleid's 4-6-2s in the 1940s. The later Maunsell locos had modified cabs to suit the Eastern Section loading gauge, and the class members were fitted with either inside bearing eight wheeled tenders, bogie tenders, or, (for the Central Section), six wheeled tenders. The naming of the class after the 'King Arthur' legend was a Public Relations coup for the Southern, and when withdrawn, 20 names were perpetuated on B.R. 5MT 4-6-0s.

Loco Weight : 79t 18c - 81t 17c *Driving Wheels :* 6' 7" *Cylinders :* (O) 20½" x 28" - 22" x 28"
Valve Gear : Walschaerts (Piston Valves)

Number Series

30448 - 30457, 30736 - 30755, 30763 - 30806

Total 74

N15X — Maunsell Rebuild — 4-6-0

Originally built by Billinton for London, Brighton & South Coast Railway as 'L' Class 4-6-4Ts, and rebuilt by Maunsell from 1934 as 4-6-0s. No. 32333 was the official L.B. & S.C.R. WW1 War Memorial loco., as No. 333 REMEMBRANCE.

Loco Weight : 73t 2c *Driving Wheels :* 6' 9" *Cylinders :* (O) 21" x 28" *Valve Gear :* Walschaerts (Piston Valves)

Number Series

32327 - 32333

Total 7

H15 — L.S.W.R. Urie / Maunsell — 4-6-0

Originally introduced by Urie in 1914 for the L.S.W.R., further additions were made by rebuilding the four cylinder E14 Class in 1915, and later by Maunsell as both new construction and the rebuilding of the four cylinder F13 Class.

Loco Weight : 79t 19c - 82t 1c *Driving Wheels :* 6' 0" *Cylinders :* (O) 21" x 28" *Valve Gear :* Walschaerts (Piston Valves)

Number Series

30330 - 30335, 30473 - 30478, 30482 - 30491, 30521 - 30524

Total 26

S15 — L.S.W.R. Urie / Maunsell — 4-6-0

Originally introduced by Urie in 1920 as a mixed traffic version of the N15s (later King Arthurs) for the L.S.W.R., further additions, with modifications, were made by Maunsell from 1927.

Loco Weight : 79t 5c - 80t 14c *Driving Wheels :* 5' 7" *Cylinders :* (O) 20½" x 28" - 21" x 28" *Valve Gear :* Walschaerts (Piston Valves)

Number Series

30496 - 30515, 30823 - 30847

Total 45

T14 — L.S.W.R. Drummond — 4-6-0

Introduced in 1911 by Drummond for the L.S.W.R., rebuilt both by Urie and Maunsell.

Loco Weight : 76t 10c *Driving Wheels :* 6' 7" *Cylinders :* (4) 15" x 26" *Valve Gear :* Walschaerts (Slide Valves)

Number Series

30443 - 30447, 30459 - 30462

Total 9

H1 — L.B.S.C.R. Marsh — 4-4-2

Introduced in 1905 by Marsh. **32039** was rebuilt with Bulleid sleeve valves in 1947

Loco Weight : 68t 5c *Driving Wheels :* 6' 7½" *Cylinders :* (O) 19" x 26" *Valve Gear :* Stephenson (Slide Valves)

Number Series

32037 - 32039

Total 3

H2 — L.B.S.C.R. Marsh — 4-4-2

Introduced in 1911 by Marsh. Superheated development of Class H1 with larger cylinders.

Loco Weight : 68t 5c *Driving Wheels :* 6' 7½" *Cylinders :* (O) 21" x 26" *Valve Gear :* Stephenson (Piston Valves)

Number Series

32421 - 32426

Total 6

B1   S.E.C.R. Wainwright   4-4-0

South Eastern Railway Class 'B', rebuilt from 1910 by Wainwright for the South Eastern & Chatham Railway

Loco Weight: 45t 2c *Driving Wheels:* 7' 0" *Cylinders:* (I) 18" x 26" *Valve Gear:* Stephenson (Slide Valves)

Number Series

31013, 31217, 31440/3/5/6/8-55/7/9   **Total 16**

B4 & B4X   L.B.S.C.R. Billinton   4-4-0

B4 : R.J. Billinton L.B.S.C. design, introduced 1899

Loco Weight: 51t 10c *Driving Wheels:* 6' 9" *Cylinders:* (I) 19" x 26" *Valve Gear:* Stephenson (Slide Valves)

B4X : L.B. Billinton L.B.S.C. design, introduced 1922, incorporating parts from B4 class

Loco Weight: 51t 10c *Driving Wheels:* 6' 9" *Cylinders:* (I) 19" x 26" *Valve Gear:* Stephenson (Slide Valves)

Number Series

B4 : 32044/51/54/62/63/68/74   **Total 7**
B4 X: 32043/45/50/52/55/56/60/67/70-73   **Total 12**

D & D1   S.E.C.R. Wainwright / Maunsell   4-4-0

D : 1901 Wainwright design for S.E.C.R.

Loco Weight: 50t 0c *Driving Wheels:* 6' 8" *Cylinders:* (I) 19" x 26" *Valve Gear:* Stephenson (Slide Valves)

D1 : Maunsell 1921 rebuild of D Class with superheated Belpaire firebox and long travel valves.

Loco Weight: 52t 4c *Driving Wheels:* 6' 8" *Cylinders:* (I) 19" x 26" *Valve Gear:* Stephenson (Slide Valves)

Number Series

D : 31057/75/92, 31477/88/90/3/6, 31501/49/74/7/86/91, 31728 - 31734, 31737/8/40/4/6/8/50   **Total 28**
D1 : 31145, 31246/7, 31470/87/9/92/4, 31502/5/9/45, 31727/35/6/9/41/3/5/9   **Total 20**

D15   L.S.W.R. Drummond   4-4-0

Introduced by Drummond in 1912 for L.S.W.R., later fitted with superheaters by Urie.
(30)463 was converted to oil burning in 1947, but reconverted to coal burning.

Loco Weight: 61t 11c *Driving Wheels:* 6' 7" *Cylinders:* (I) 20" x 26" *Valve Gear:* Walschaerts (Piston Valves)

Number Series

30463 - 30472

                     Total 10

E & E1   S.E.C.R. Wainwright / Maunsell   4-4-0

E : 1905 Wainwright design for S.E.C.R.

Loco Weight: 52t 5c *Driving Wheels:* 6' 6" *Cylinders:* (I) 19" x 26" *Valve Gear:* Stephenson (Slide Valves)

E1 : Maunsell 1919 rebuild of E Class with larger superheated Belpaire firebox & long travel valves.

Loco Weight: 53t 9c *Driving Wheels:* 6' 6" *Cylinders:* (I) 19" x 26" *Valve Gear:* Stephenson (Piston Valves)

Number Series

E : 31036, 31157/9/66/75/6, 31273/5, 31315, 31491, 31514 - 31516, 31447/87   **Total 15**
E1: 31019/67, 31160/3/5/79, 31497, 31504/6/7/11   **Total 11**

F1   S.E.C.R. Wainwright   4-4-0

1903 Wainwright rebuild of Stirling Class F, originally built for South Eastern Railway.

Loco Weight: 45t 2c *Driving Wheels:* 7' 0" *Cylinders:* (I) 18" x 26" *Valve Gear:* Stephenson (Slide Valves)

Number Series

31002/28/31/42/78, 31105/51, 31215/31

                   Total 9

K10   L.S.W.R Drummond   4-4-0

Introduced in 1901 by Drummond for L.S.W.R.

Loco Weight: 46t 14c   *Driving Wheels:* 5' 7"   *Cylinders:* (I) 18½" x 26"   *Valve Gear:* Stephenson (Slide Valves)

Number Series

30135/7/9,   30140 - 30146,   30150 - 30153,   30329,   30340/1/3/5,   30380/2 - 30386,   30389 - 30394

Total 31

L   S.E.C.R. Wainwright   4-4-0

Introduced in 1914 by Wainwright for South Eastern & Chatham Railway. 31772— 31781 were built by Borsig of Berlin, and delivered just before the outbreak of the First World War in 1914.

Loco Weight: 57t 9c *Driving Wheels:* 6' 8"   *Cylinders:* (I) 19½" x 26" *Valve Gear:* Stephenson (Piston Valves)

Number Series

31760 - 31781

Total 22

L1   S.R. Maunsell   4-4-0

Maunsell design for the Southern Railway, introduced in 1926. Very similar to the 'D1' and 'E1' classes in appearance, the 'L1s' were a development of Class L (above)

Loco Weight: 57t 16c *Driving Wheels:* 6' 8"   *Cylinders:* (I) 19½" x 26" *Valve Gear:* Stephenson (Piston Valves)

Number Series

31753 - 31759,   31782 - 31789

Total 15

L11   L.S.W.R Drummond   4-4-0

1903 introduction by Drummond, a development of his K10 class with T9 boiler & larger firebox.

Loco Weight: 50t 11c *Driving Wheels:* 5' 7"   *Cylinders:* (I) 18½" x 26" *Valve Gear:* Stephenson (Slide Valves)

Number Series

30134,   30148,   30154 - 30159,   30161,   30163 - 30175,   30405 - 30414,   30435 - 30447

Total 45

L12   L.S.W.R Drummond   4-4-0

Drummond development of T9 with larger boiler, superheated by Urie from 1915

Loco Weight: 55t 5c   *Driving Wheels:* 6' 7"   *Cylinders:* (I) 10" x 26" *Valve Gear:* Stephenson (Slide Valves)

Number Series

30415 - 30434

Total 20

S11   L.S.W.R Drummond   4-4-0

Introduced in 1903 by Drummond as a smaller wheeled development of the T9 Class (see below)

Loco Weight: 53t 15c *Driving Wheels:* 6' 0"   *Cylinders:* (I) 19" x 26" *Valve Gear:* Stephenson (Slide Valves)

Number Series

30395 - 30404

Total 10

T9   L.S.W.R Drummond   4-4-0

Introduced in 1899 by Drummond, fitted with larger cylinders & superheater by Urie from 1922.
Nos **30300-305/7/10-14/36-8** were introduced in 1900 with full width splashers and cab.
Locos were either fitted with eight wheeled tenders with inside bearings (nicknamed 'watercarts'), or with more conventional six wheeled tenders. The 'Watercart' tenders were also used on other L.S.W.R. 4-4-0s and 4-6-0s including the 'King Arthur' class locos,

Loco Weight: 51t 7c - 51t 18c *Driving Wheels:* 6' 7"   *Cylinders:* (I)19" x 26" *Valve Gear:* Stephenson (Slide Valves)

Number Series

30113 - 30122,   30280 - 30289,   30300 - 30305,   30307,   30310 - 30314,   30336 - 30338,   30702 - 30719, 30721 - 30733

Total 66

V 'Schools'   S.R. Maunsell   4-4-0

An extremely powerful 4-4-0, introduced by Maunsell in 1930. Bulleid modified nos. **30900/1/7/13 - 15/7-21/4/9 -31/3/4/7-9** with multiple jet blastpipes & larger diameter chimneys from 1938 onwards.

Loco Weight : 67t 2c _Driving Wheels :_ 6' 7" _Cylinders :_ (3) 16½" x 26" _Valve Gear :_ Walschaerts (Piston Valves)

Number Series

30900 - 30939   _Total 40_

K   L.B.S.C.R. Billinton   2-6-0

L.B. Billinton design for L.B.S.C.R., introduced 1913.

Loco Weight : 63t 15c _Driving Wheels :_ 5' 7" _Cylinders :_ (O) 21" x 26" _Valve Gear :_ Stephenson (Piston Valves)

Number Series

32337 - 32353   _Total 17_

N & N1   S.E.C.R. Maunsell   2-6-0

N :   Introduced by Maunsell in 1917 for the S.E.C.R. as a mixed traffic design.

Loco Weight : 61t 4c _Driving Wheels :_ 5' 6" _Cylinders :_ (O) 19" x 28" _Valve Gear :_ Walschaerts (Piston Valves)

N1 : Three cylinder development of Class N, introduced 1922

Loco Weight : 64t 5c _Driving Wheels :_ 5' 6" _Cylinders :_ (3) 16" x 28" _Valve Gear :_ Walschaerts (Piston Valves)

Number Series

N : 31400 - 31414, 31810 - 31821, 31823 - 31875   _Total 80_
N1 : 31822, 31876 - 31880   _Total 6_

U & U1   S.R. Maunsell   2-6-0

U :   Introduced by Maunsell in 1928; Some were rebuilt from 'River' Class 2-6-4Ts (**31790 - 31809**)

Loco Weight : 63t 0c _Driving Wheels :_ 6' 0" _Cylinders :_ (O) 19" x 28" _Valve Gear :_ Walschaerts (Piston Valves)

U1 : 1928 three cylinder rebuild of Class U 2-6-4T, originally introduced 1925. **31891 - 31910** were Introduced in 1928 to the same design as the rebuilds, but with smaller splashers.

Loco Weight : 65t 6c _Driving Wheels :_ 6' 0" _Cylinders :_ (3) 16" x 28" _Valve Gear :_ Walschaerts (Piston Valves)

Number Series

U : 31610 - 31639, 31790 - 31809   _Total 50_
U1 : 31890 - 31910   _Total 21_

C   S.E.C.R. Wainwright   0-6-0

Wainwright design for S.E.C.R., introduced 1900.

Loco Weight : 43t 16c _Driving Wheels :_ 5' 2" _Cylinders :_ (I) 18½" x 26" _Valve Gear :_ Stephenson (Slide Valves)

Number Series

31004/18/33/7/8/54/9/61/3/8/71/86/90, 31102/12/3/50/91, 31218/9/21/3/5/7/9/34/42-5/52/3/5-7/60/7/8/7/
91/3/4/7/8, 31317, 31460/1/80/1/6/95/8, 31508/10/3/72/3/5/6/8-85/8-90/2/3, 31681-4/6-95,
31711 - 31725

                                                                                Total 106

C2   L.B.S.C.R. Billinton   0-6-0

Introduced 1893, R.J. Billinton design for L.B.S.C.R.

Loco Weight : 39t 10c _Driving Wheels :_ 5' 0" _Cylinders :_ (I) 17½" x 26" _Valve Gear :_ Stephenson (Slide Valves)

Number Series

32435/6, 32533

                                                                                Total 3

C2X   L.B.S.C.R. Marsh   0-6-0

Marsh design for L.B.S.C.R., introduced in 1908. Rebuild of C2 with larger C3 boiler

Loco Weight: 45t 5c   *Driving Wheels:* 5' 0"   *Cylinders:* (I) 17½" x 26"   *Valve Gear:* Stephenson (Slide Valves)

Number Series

32434/7/8, 32440 - 32451, 32521 - 32529, 32532, 32534 - 32541, 32543 - 32554

Total 45

C3   L.B.S.C.R. Marsh   0-6-0

Marsh design for L.B.S.C.R., introduced in 1906.

Loco Weight: 47t 10c   *Driving Wheels:* 5' 0"   *Cylinders:* (I) 17½" x 26"   *Valve Gear:* Stephenson (Slide Valves)

Number Series

32300 - 32303, 32306 - 32309

Total 8

O1   S.E.C.R. Wainwright   0-6-0

Introduced by Wainwright in 1903, these engines were a rebuild of Stirling's S.E.R. 'O' Class.

Loco Weight: 41t 1c   *Driving Wheels:* 5' 2"   *Cylinders:* (I) 18" x 26"   *Valve Gear:* Stephenson (Slide Valves)

Number Series

31003/7/14/39/41/4/6/8/51/64/5/6/80/93, 31106/8/9/23, 31238/48/58, 31316/69/70-4/7-81/3-6/8-91/5-8, 31425/6/8-30/2/4/7-9

Total 55

Q   S.R. Maunsell   0-6-0

Maunsell design for Southern Railway, introduced in 1938. Only 20 were built, as the design was superseded by Bulleid's much more powerful class Q1 (see below)

Loco Weight: 49t 10c   *Driving Wheels:* 5' 1"   *Cylinders:* (I) 19" x 26"   *Valve Gear:* Stephenson (Piston Valves)

Number Series

30530 - 30549

Total 20

Q1   S.R. Bulleid   0-6-0

Bulleid wartime austerity design for Southern Railway.

Loco Weight: 49t 10c   *Driving Wheels:* 5' 1"   *Cylinders:* (I) 19" x 26"   *Valve Gear:* Stephenson (Piston Valves)

Number Series

33001 - 33040 (formerly S.R. C1 - C40)

Total 40

---

700   L.S.W.R. Drummond   0-6-0

1897 Drummond design, fitted with superheaters from 1921

Loco Weight: 46t 14c   *Driving Wheels:* 5' 1"   *Cylinders:* (I) 19" x 26"   *Valve Gear:* Stephenson (Slide Valves)

Number Series

30306/8/9/15-7/39/46/50/2/5/68, 30687 - 30701

Total 30

0395   L.S.W.R. Adams   0-6-0

Introduced in 1881 by Adams for the London & South Western Railway.

Loco Weight: 37t 12c - 38t 14c   *Driving Wheels:* 5' 1"   *Cylinders:* (I) 19" x 26"   *Valve Gear:* Stephenson (Slide Valves)

Number Series

30564 - 30581

Total 18

A12　　　　　L.S.W.R. Adams　　　　　0-4-2
1887 design by Adams for the London & South Western Railway
Loco Weight: 42t 7c *Driving Wheels:* 6' 0"　*Cylinders:* (I) 18" x 26"　*Valve Gear:* Stephenson (Slide Valves)

Number Series
30612/8/27/9/36　　　　　　　　　　　　　　　　　　　　　*Total 5*

'Leader'　　　　　S.R. Bulleid　　　　　0-6-6-0
One of the most unconventional steam locomotives ever built, this double ended design with central boiler was designed by O.V. Bulleid for the Southern Railway, but the first one wasn't completed until after Nationalisation, and ran trials for almost 18 months. These showed major problems, not the least being the high temperatures and cramped conditions the fireman had to work in.
Six locomotives were ordered, but only two were completed and only one (**36001**) was steamed.

Number Series
36001 - 36006　　　　　　　　　　　　　　　　　　　　　*Total 6*

G16　　　　　L.S.W.R. Urie　　　　　4-8-0T
1921 Urie design for 'hump' shunting.
Loco Weight: 95t 2c *Driving Wheels:* 5' 1"　*Cylinders:* (O) 22" x 28"　*Valve Gear:* Walschaerts (Piston Valves)

Number Series
30492 - 30495　　　　　　　　　　　　　　　　　　　　　*Total 4*

H16　　　　　L.S.W.R. Urie　　　　　4-6-2T
Introduced by Urie in 1921 for heavy transfer freight work.
Loco Weight: 96t 8c *Driving Wheels:* 5' 7"　*Cylinders:* (O) 21" x 28"　*Valve Gear:* Walschaerts (Piston Valves)

Number Series
30516 - 30520　　　　　　　　　　　　　　　　　　　　　*Total 5*

J1　　　　　L.B.S.C.R. Marsh　　　　　4-6-2T
1910 design by Marsh for L.B.S.C.R.
Loco Weight: 89t 0c *Driving Wheels:* 6' 7"　*Cylinders:* (O) 21" x 26"　*Valve Gear:* Stephenson (Piston Valves)

Number Series
32325　　　　　　　　　　　　　　　　　　　　　　　　*Total 1*

J2　　　　　L.B.S.C.R. Billinton　　　　　4-6-2T
1910 design by Marsh for L.B.S.C.R.
Loco Weight: 89t 0c *Driving Wheels:* 6' 7"　*Cylinders:* (O) 21" x 26"　*Valve Gear:* Walschaerts (Piston Valves)

Number Series
32326　　　　　　　　　　　　　　　　　　　　　　　　*Total 1*

I1X　　　　　Maunsell Rebuild　　　　　4-4-2T
Maunsell 1925 rebuild of Marsh LBSCR I1 Class. 2001 - 2010 rebuilt 1929 with shorter wheelbase.
Loco Weight: 71t 18c *Driving Wheels:* 5' 6"　*Cylinders:* (I) 17½" x 26"　*Valve Gear:* Stephenson (Slide Valves)

Number Series
32001 - 32010, 32595/6/8/9, 32601 - 32604　　　　　　　　　　*Total 18*

I3   L.B.S.C.R. Marsh / Billinton   4-4-2T

32021 was introduced in 1907 by Marsh, later rebuilt with superheater & extended smokebox.
Loco Weight : 75t 10c *Driving Wheels :* 6' 9" *Cylinders :* (I) 19" x 26" *Valve Gear :* Stephenson (Slide Valves)

32022/3/5-30/75-81 were introduced in 1908 by Marsh with smaller wheels and piston valves.
These locos were later superheated.
Loco Weight : 76t 0c *Driving Wheels :* 6' 7½" *Cylinders :* (I) 20" x 26" *Valve Gear :* Stephenson (Piston Valves)

32082 - 32091 were introduced in 1912 by L.B. Billinton, and were fitted with superheaters and
larger cylinders.
Loco Weight : 76t 0c *Driving Wheels :* 6' 7½" *Cylinders :* (I) 21" x 26" *Valve Gear :* Stephenson (Piston Valves)

Number Series

32021-3/5-30/75-91

Total 26

0415   L.S.W.R. Adams   4-4-2T

Adams design of 1882 for L.S.W.R.

Loco Weight : 55t 2c *Driving Wheels :* 5' 7" *Cylinders :* (O) 17½" x 24" *Valve Gear :* Stephenson (Slide Valves)

Number Series

30582 - 30584

Total 3

W   S.R. Maunsell   2-6-4T

Maunsell tank version of N1 class 2-6-0, introduced 1931

Loco Weight : 90t 14c *Driving Wheels :* 5' 6" *Cylinders :* (3) 16½" x 28" *Valve Gear :* Walschaerts (Piston Valves)

Number Series

31911 - 31925

Total 25

0298   L.S.W.R. Beattie   2-4-0WT

1863 Beattie design for L.S.W.R., rebuilt by Adams, Urie, and Maunsell, over the years.

Loco Weight : 37t 16c *Driving Wheels :* 5' 7" *Cylinders :* (O) 16½" x 20" *Valve Gear :* Stephenson (Slide Valves)

Number Series

30585 - 30587

Total 3

Hawthorn Leslie   K. & E.S.R.   0-8-0T

Hawthorn Leslie design for Kent & East Sussex Railway, built 1904. Obtained in 1932 by Southern
Railway, and later rebuilt with L.B.S.C.R. boiler.

Loco Weight : 47t 10c *Driving Wheels :* 4' 3" *Cylinders :* (O) 16" x 24" *Valve Gear :* Stephenson (Slide Valves)

Number Series

30949

Total 1

Z   S.R. Maunsell   0-8-0T

Introduced in 1929 by Maunsell for heavy shunting work.

Loco Weight : 71t 12c *Driving Wheels:* 4' 8½" *Cylinders :* (3) 16" x 28" *Valve Gear :* Walschaerts (Piston Valves)

Number Series

30950 - 30957

Total 8

J   S.E.C.R. Wainwright   0-6-4T

Introduced by Wainwright in 1913.

Loco Weight : 70t 4c *Driving Wheels :* 5' 6" *Cylinders :* (O) 19½" x 26" *Valve Gear :* Stephenson (Piston Valves)

Number Series

31595 - 31599

Total 5

E1R   Maunsell Rebuild   0-6-2T

Introduced in 1927. Maunsell rebuild of Class E1 0-6-0T with trailing axle and larger bunker, for service in the West of England.

Loco Weight : 50t 5c *Driving Wheels :* 4' 6" *Cylinders :* (I) 17" x 24" *Valve Gear :* Stephenson (Slide Valves)

Number Series

32094 - 6, 32124/35, 32608/10/95 - 7

Total 10

E3   L.B.S.C.R. Billinton   0-6-2T

Introduced in 1894 by R.J. Billinton. Reboilered and fitted with extended smokeboxes from 1918.

Loco Weight : 56t 10c *Driving Wheels :* 4' 6" *Cylinders :* (I) 17½" x 26" *Valve Gear :* Stephenson (Slide Valves)

Number Series

32165 - 32170, 32453 - 32462

Total 16

E4   L.B.S.C.R. Billinton   0-6-2T

1897 design by R.J. Billinton, fitted with new boilers & extended smokeboxes from 1910.

Loco Weight : 57t 10c *Driving Wheels :* 5' 0" *Cylinders :* (I) 17½" x 26" *Valve Gear :* Stephenson (Slide Valves)

Number Series

32463-5/7-76/9-82/4-8/90-9, 32500-20/56-66/77-82

Total 70

E4X   L.B.S.C.R. Marsh   0-6-2T

Introduced in 1909 by Marsh, these locos were reboilered E4s with I2 class boilers.

Loco Weight : 59t 5c *Driving Wheels :* 5' 0" *Cylinders :* (I) 17½" x 26" *Valve Gear :* Stephenson (Slide Valves)

Number Series

32466/77/8/89

Total 4

E5   L.B.S.C.R. Billinton   0-6-2T

Introduced in 1902. R.J. Billinton design

Loco Weight : 60t 0c *Driving Wheels :* 5' 6" *Cylinders :* (I) 17½" x 26" *Valve Gear :* Stephenson (Slide Valves)

Number Series

32399, 32400/2/4 - 6, 32567/8/71 - 5/83 - 5/7 - 94

Total 24

E5X   L.B.S.C.R. Marsh   0-6-2T

Introduced in 1911. L.B. Billinton rebuild of Class E5 with larger boiler.

Loco Weight : 64t 5c *Driving Wheels :* 5' 6" *Cylinders :* (I) 17½" x 26" *Valve Gear :* Stephenson (Slide Valves)

Number Series

32401, 32570/6/86

Total 4

E6   L.B.S.C.R. Billinton   0-6-2T

Introduced 1904 by R.J. Billinton
Loco Weight: 61t 0c   *Driving Wheels:* 4' 6"   *Cylinders:* (I) 18" x 26"   *Valve Gear:* Stephenson (Slide Valves)

Number Series

32408 - 10/2 - 8   **Total 10**

E6X   L.B.S.C.R. Marsh   0-6-2T

Class E6X rebuilt from 1911 with 'C3' boiler
Loco Weight: 63t 0c   *Driving Wheels:* 4' 6"   *Cylinders:* (I) 18" x 26"   *Valve Gear:* Stephenson (Slide Valves)

Number Series

32407/11   **Total 2**

Hawthorn Leslie   P.D.S.W.J.R.   0-6-2T

Introduced in 1907 by Hawthorn Leslie & Co. for P.D.S.W.J.R.
Loco Weight: 49t 19c *Driving Wheels:* 4' 0"   *Cylinders:* (O) 16" x 24" *Valve Gear:* Stephenson (Slide Valves)

Number Series

30757/8   **Total 2**

A1 & A1X   L.B.S.C.R. Stroudley   0-6-0T

A class of fifty locomotives introduced by William Stroudley in 1872, originally Class A1, most were
rebuilt with extended smokeboxes as class A1X, and the only A1 to survive into B.R. days was
DS680. Several were sold to other railways before the 1923 grouping, and two which were sold to
the W.C.P.R. are dealt with in BOOK ONE of this series, as they became G.W.R. stock. (B.R. Nos.
4 & 5). They were tiny, powerful, quaint, and utterly lovable! 32636 had larger cylinders.
Some were used over the years on the Isle of Wight, and others became Departmental locomotives
Loco Weight: 27t 10c - 28t 5c *Driving Wheels:* 4' 0" *Cylinders:* (I) 12" x 20" *Valve Gear:* Stephenson (Slide Valves)

Number Series

**DS680, DS377 (renumbered 32635), 32636, DS515 (renumbered 32650), 32640/4/7/55,
32659 (renumbered DS681), 32661/2, 32662, 32678, W8 (renumbered 32646),
W13 (renumbered 32677), Kent & East Sussex 3 (renumbered 32670)**   **Total 15**

E1   L.B.S.C.R. Stroudley   0-6-0T

Stroudley 1874 design for L.B.S.C.R., later rebuilt by Marsh.
W1 - W4 are fitted with Westinghouse brake gear.
Loco Weight: 44t 3c   *Driving Wheels:* 4' 6"   *Cylinders:* (I) 17" x 24" *Valve Gear:* Stephenson (Slide Valves)

Number Series

W1 - W4, 32097, 32112/3/22/22/7-9/33/8/9/41/2/5/7/51/3/6/60/2/4, 32606/9/89-91/4   **Total 30**

E2   L.B.S.C.R. Billinton   0-6-0T

Introduced in 1913 by L.B. Billinton for the London, Brighton & South Coast Railway.
Loco nos. 32105 - 32109 had extended side tanks, and were introduced in 1915.
Loco Weight: 52t 15c *Driving Wheels:* 4' 6"   *Cylinders:* (I) 17½" x 26" *Valve Gear:* Stephenson (Slide Valves)
(Numbers **32105 - 32109** weighed 15c more because of the extended side tanks.)

Number Series

32100 - 32109   **Total 10**

0330   K.E.S.R. (ex L.S.W.R.)   0-6-0ST

1876 design for L.S.W.R., built by Beyer Peacock. No. 0335 to K.E.S.R. in 1932 in exchange for **(30)949**
Loco Weight: 34t 19½c *Driving Wheels:* 4' 3"   *Cylinders:* (I) 17" x 24"   *Valve Gear:* Stephenson (Slide Valves)

Number Series

K.E.S.R. 4 (B.R. Number not allocated)   **Total 1**

Kerr Stuart   East Kent Railway   0-6-0T

Kerr Stuart design for East Kent Railway, built in 1917. Became EKR Number 4 and passed to British Railways on Nationalisation.

Loco Weight: 40t 0c   *Driving Wheels:* 5' 7"   *Cylinders:* (I) 17" x 24"   *Valve Gear:* Stephenson (Slide Valves)

Number Series

30948 (EKR 4)

Total 1

G6   L.S.W.R. Adams   0-6-0T

Introduced 1894 by Adams for L.S.W.R.
Numbers (30)160, (30)259 & (30)274 were fitted with Drummond type boilers from 1925 onwards.

Loco Weight: 47t 13c   *Driving Wheels:* 4' 10"   *Cylinders:* (I) 17½" x 24"   *Valve Gear:* Stephenson (Slide Valves)

Number Series

30160/2, 30237 - 30240, 30257 - 30279, 30348/9/51/3/4.

Total 34

P   S.E.C.R. Wainwright   0-6-0T

Originally introduced by Wainwright as Auto Train locos in 1909, these extremely small engines were later used for shunting, particularly on light track and sharp curves.

Loco Weight: 28t 10c   *Driving Wheels:* 3' 9"   *Cylinders:* (I) 12" x 18"   *Valve Gear:* Stephenson (Slide Valves)

Number Series

31027, 31178, 31323/5, 31555 - 31558

Total 8

R1   S.E.C.R. Stirling   0-6-0T

Stirling design for South Eastern Railway, introduced in 1888.

Loco Weight: 46t 15c   *Driving Wheels:* 5' 2"   *Cylinders:* (I) 18" x 26"   *Valve Gear:* Stephenson (Slide Valves)

From 1938 nos.(3)1010/69, (3)1107/47 & (3)1339 were fitted with cut down cab, chimney and boiler fittings for use on the Canterbury and Whitstable branch.

Loco Weight: 46t 8c   *Driving Wheels:* 5' 1"   *Cylinders:* (I) 18" x 26"   *Valve Gear:* Stephenson (Slide Valves)

Number Series

31010/47/69, 31107/27/8/47/54/74, 31335/7/9/40

Total 13

S   S.E.C.R. Wainwright   0-6-0ST

1917 rebuild by Maunsell of Wainwright Class C 0-6-0

Loco Weight: 53t 10c   *Driving Wheels:* 5' 2"   *Cylinders:* (I) 18½" x 26"   *Valve Gear:* Stephenson (Slide Valves)

Number Series

31685

Total 1

T   S.E.C.R. Kirtley   0-6-0T

Introduced in 1879 by Kirtley for the London, Chatham & Dover Railway

Loco Weight: 40t 15c   *Driving Wheels:* 4' 6"   *Cylinders:* (I) 17½" x 24"   *Valve Gear:* Stephenson (Slide Valves)

Number Series

500S, 31602/4

Total 3

USA — Southern Railway — 0-6-0T

Typically American design of switcher (shunter), brought to this country by the United States Transportation Corps for eventual war service in Europe. Fourteen were purchased by the Southern Railway for shunting at Southampton Docks, and were fitted with modified cabs, bunkers, and British style buffers and drawgear. A fifteenth loco was purchased for spares but wasn't taken into stock. They were powerful and sturdy locos, and several were transferred to departmental service when displaced by diesel shunters at Southampton Docks.

Loco Weight: 46t 10c *Driving Wheels:* 4' 6" *Cylinders:* (O) 16½" x 24" *Valve Gear:* Walschaerts (Piston Valves)

Number Series

30061 - 30074   *Total 14*

Hawthorn Leslie — P.D.S.W.J.R. — 0-6-0T

Hawthorn Leslie design for Plymouth, Devonport and South Western Junction Railway. Built 1907

Loco Weight: 35t 15c *Driving Wheels:* 3' 10" *Cylinders:* (O) 14" x 22" *Valve Gear:* Stephenson (Slide Valves)

Number Series

30756   *Total 1*

D3 & D3X — L.B.S.C.R. Billinton — 0-4-4T

D3 Class introduced in 1892 by R.J. Billinton, later reboilered and fitted with push pull equipment. 32397 was Class D3X, rebuilt from Class D3 by Marsh in 1909, and weighed 53t 0c

Loco Weight: 52t 0c *Driving Wheels:* 5' 6" *Cylinders:* (I) 17½" x 26" *Valve Gear:* Stephenson (Slide Valves)

Number Series

32364-8/70-4/6-80/3-91/3-5/7/8

Total 29

H — S.E.C.R. Wainwright — 0-4-4T

Wainwright design, introduced in 1904

Loco Weight: 54t 8c *Driving Wheels:* 5' 6" *Cylinders:* (I) 18" x 26" *Valve Gear:* Stephenson (Slide Valves)

Number Series

31005/16/158/61/2/4/77/82/4/93/239/59/61/3/5/6/69/74/6/8/9/95, 31305 - 31311, 31319 - 31322/4, 31326 - 31329, 31500/3/12/17 - 23/30 - 3/40 - 44/6/8/50 - 54

Total 64

M7 — L.S.W.R. Drummond — 0-4-4T

The original 'M7' design was introduced by Drummond in 1897, and was added to in 1903 by the introduction of the 'X14' class, which had steam reversers and increased overhangs. The 'X14' class was later incorporated into 'M7'. After 1925, many were fitted with push pull equipment.

Loco Weight: 60t 4c - 62t 0c *Driving Wheels:* 5' 7" *Cylinders:* (I) 18½" x 26" *Valve Gear:* Stephenson (Slide Valves)

Number Series

30021 - 30060, 30104 - 30112, 30123 - 30133, 30241 - 30256, 30318 - 30324/8/56/7, 30374 - 30379, 30479/80/1, 30667 - 30676   *Total 104*

O2 — L.S.W.R. Adams — 0-4-4T

Adams design for L.S.W.R., introduced in 1889. After 1923, some were rebuilt with larger bunkers and fitted with Westinghouse air brakes for service on the Isle of Wight.

Loco Weight: 46t 18c - 48t 8c *Driving Wheels:* 4' 10" *Cylinders:* (I) 17½" x 24" *Valve Gear:* Stephenson (Slide Valves)

Number Series

30177/9/81 (later W35), 30182/3/92/3/7/8 (later W36), 30199, 30200/3/4/7/12/3/6/21/3/4/5, 30229 - 30233, 30236, W14 - W36   *Total 48*

R   S.E.C.R. Kirtley   0-4-4T

Introduced during 1891 by Kirtley for the London, Chatham and Dover Railway. Later rebuilt with 'H' Class boilers.

Loco Weight: 48t 15c *Driving Wheels:* 5' 6" *Cylinders:* (I) 17½" x 24" *Valve Gear:* Stephenson (Slide Valves)

Number Series

31658 - 31663, 31665 - 31667, 31670 - 31675

Total 15

R1   S.E.C.R. Kirtley   0-4-4T

A 1900 development of Class 'R' (above) with enlarged bunkers, delivered to the newly formed South Eastern & Chatham Railway. All later rebuilt with 'H' Class boilers.

Loco Weight: 52t 3c *Driving Wheels:* 5' 6" *Cylinders:* (I) 17½" x 24" *Valve Gear:* Stephenson (Slide Valves)

Number Series

31696 - 31700, 31703 - 31710

Total 13

T1   L.S.W.R. Adams   0-4-4T

Introduced by Adams in 1894. Originally Class 'F6', but later incorporated into 'T1' Class.

Loco Weight: 57t 2c *Driving Wheels:* 5' 7" *Cylinders:* (I) 18" x 26" *Valve Gear:* Stephenson (Slide Valves)

Number Series

30001/2/3/5/7 - 10/3/20, 30361/3/6/7

Total 14

D1 & D1M   L.B.S.C.R. Stroudley   0-4-2T

D1 :   Stroudley 1873 design for the L.B.S.C.R.
D1M :   Fitted with Push pull equipment from 1909.

Loco Weight: 43t 10c *Driving Wheels:* 5' 6" *Cylinders:* (I) 17" x 24" *Valve Gear:* Stephenson (Slide Valves)

Number Series

D1 : 32286, 32359   *Total 2*
D1M : 32215/34/5/9/52/3/9/69/74/83/9/99, 32358/61, 32605/99, 700S, 701S   *Total 18*

B4   L.S.W.R. Adams   0-4-0T

Introduced in 1891 for the L.& S.W.R. by Adams. Originally designed for dock shunting, many were used at Southampton Docks until displaced by the 'USA' class 0-6-0Ts purchased from the United States Army after the Second World War. **30082-4 & 30101** were originally Class K14 with smaller boiler & altered fittings, and many of the class were named after French Ports until Nationalisation.

Loco Weight: 79t 5c *Driving Wheels:* 5' 7" *Cylinders:* (O) 20½" x 28" *Valve Gear:* Stephenson (Slide Valves)

Number Series

30081 - 30103, 30147, 30176

Total 25

C14   L.S.W.R. Drummond / Urie   0-4-0T

Originally introduced by Drummond as 2-2-0Ts for motor train working, rebuilt in 1913 by Urie as 0-4-0Ts.

Loco Weight: 25t 15c *Driving Wheels:* 3' 0" *Cylinders:* (O) 14" x 14" *Valve Gear:* Stephenson (Slide Valves)

Number Series

77S, 30588/9

Total 3

Crane Tank   S.E.C.R.   0-4-0CT

Neilson crane tank design for London, Chatham & Dover Railway

Loco Weight : 17t 17c *Driving Wheels :* 3' 3" *Cylinders :* (I) 11" x 20" *Valve Gear :* Stephenson (Slide Valves)

Number Series

31302

Total 1

Hawthorn Leslie   Southampton Docks Co.   0-4-0ST

1890 design by Hawthorn Leslie for Southampton Docks Co., taken over by L.S.W.R. in 1892.

Loco Weight : 21t 2c *Driving Wheels :* 3' 2" *Cylinders :* (O) 12" x 20" *Valve Gear :* Stephenson (Slide Valves)

Number Series

30458

Total 1

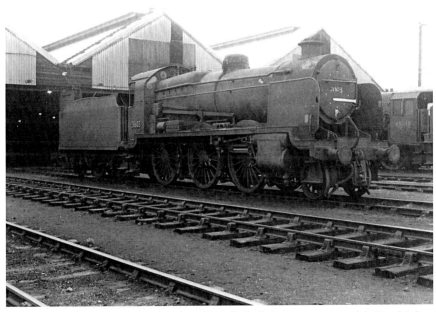

Class 'U' 2-6-0 No. 31803 (70C - Guildford) looks forlorn as it sits outside Eastleigh Shed with no valve gear or connecting rods. The missing cast smokebox number plate and the crudely painted replacement number and shedcode add to the air of desolation surrounding this former 'River' class 2-6-4T. No. 31803 was a late surviving Maunsell 2-6-0, and 'U' Class was a larger wheeled version of the far more numerous 'N' Class

Seen in the background is Stanier 'Black 5' 4-6-0 No. 45418 (2D - Banbury), possibly visiting Eastleigh Works for attention, as this was one of the last works still servicing steam locomotives; many London Midland locos visited here in the last years of steam. 'Black 5's also replaced Banbury 'Halls' on the York—Bournemouth passenger trains in the latter years of steam, so No. 45418 may have also been working this service.

SECTION TWO

Southern Region (ex Southern Railway) Locomotive Allocations

in numerical order

Number	Class	W.Arrgt.	1948	1952	1955	1959	1963	1966	w/dwn	Notes
30001	T1	0-4-4T	ELH	-	-	-	-	-	07/49	
30002	T1	0-4-4T	ELH	-	-	-	-	-	03/49	
30003	T1	0-4-4T	PLY	-	-	-	-	-	10/48	
30005	T1	0-4-4T	ELH	-	-	-	-	-	01/50	
30007	T1	0-4-4T	PLY	-	-	-	-	-	06/51	
30008	T1	0-4-4T	ELH	-	-	-	-	-	05/49	
30009	T1	0-4-4T	FEL	-	-	-	-	-	07/48	
30010	T1	0-4-4T	SAL	-	-	-	-	-	08/48	
30013	T1	0-4-4T	SAL	-	-	-	-	-	03/49	
30020	T1	0-4-4T	FRA	-	-	-	-	-	06/51	
30021	M7	0-4-4T	BM	72A	72A	72A	75F	-	03/64	Push Pull fitted
30022	M7	0-4-4T	GFD	70C	70C	-	-	-	05/58	
30023	M7	0-4-4T	BPL	72A	72A	72A	-	-	10/61	
30024	M7	0-4-4T	EXJ	72A	72A	72A	71B	-	03/63	
30025	M7	0-4-4T	EXJ	72A	72A	72A	71B	-	05/54	
30026	M7	0-4-4T	GFD	70C	70C	70C	-	-	04/59	
30027	M7	0-4-4T	FRA	70C	70C	70C	-	-	11/59	Push Pull fitted
30028	M7	0-4-4T	BM	70C	70C	71A	-	-	09/62	Push Pull fitted
30029	M7	0-4-4T	ELH	71A	71A	71A	75F	-	05/64	Push Pull fitted
30030	M7	0-4-4T	EXJ	71A	71A	71A	-	-	10/59	
30031	M7	0-4-4T	FEL	71A	71A	75A	71B	-	05/63	Push Pull fitted. Swapped identity with **30128** 01/60
30032	M7	0-4-4T	EXJ	71A	71A	71A	70B	-	07/63	
30033	M7	0-4-4T	9E	71A	71A	71A	-	-	12/62	
30034	M7	0-4-4T	EXJ	72D	72D	83H	-	-	02/63	
30035	M7	0-4-4T	PLY	72D	72D	83H	-	-	02/63	
30036	M7	0-4-4T	BPL	72D	72D	83H	71B	-	01/64	
30037	M7	0-4-4T	EXJ	72D	72D	-	-	-	05/58	
30038	M7	0-4-4T	9E	70B	70B	-	-	-	02/58	
30039	M7	0-4-4T	EXJ	72D	72D	70F	-	-	02/63	
30040	M7	0-4-4T	BM	72A	72D	71B	-	-	06/61	
30041	M7	0-4-4T	SAL	72A	70B	-	-	-	08/57	
30042	M7	0-4-4T	BPL	72A	70B	-	-	-	06/57	
30043	M7	0-4-4T	GFD	70B	70B	70B	-	-	05/61	
30044	M7	0-4-4T	BPL	72A	72A	72A	-	-	09/61	
30045	M7	0-4-4T	FRA	72A	72A	72A	-	-	12/62	Push Pull fitted
30046	M7	0-4-4T	EXJ	72A	72A	72A	-	-	02/59	" " "
30047	M7	0-4-4T	BM	75D	75D	75D	-	-	02/60	" " "
30048	M7	0-4-4T	ELH	75D	75D	75D	72A	-	01/64	" " "
30049	M7	0-4-4T	EXJ	75D	75D	75D	-	-	05/62	" " "
30050	M7	0-4-4T	BM	75D	75D	75D	-	-	01/62	" " "
30051	M7	0-4-4T	BM	71D	75D	75D	-	-	09/62	" " "
30052	M7	0-4-4T	BM	71D	75A	75A	72C	-	05/64	" " "
30053	M7	0-4-4T	ELH	71D	75A	75A	75F	-	05/64	" " "
30054	M7	0-4-4T	FRA	71D	70F	75A	-	-	01/59	" " "
30055	M7	0-4-4T	EXJ	71B	70F	75A	75F	-	09/63	" " "
30056	M7	0-4-4T	GFD	71B	71B	75A	71B	-	12/63	" " "
30057	M7	0-4-4T	BM	71B	71B	71B	71B	-	06/63	" " "

Bricklayers Arms allocated Class 'H' 0-4-4T No 31533 was withdrawn during September 1962. these were competent little engines which gave sterling service on the Southern for many years.

King Arthur Class 'N15' 4-6-0 No 30782 'Sir Brian', a Bournemouth based loco during B.R. days, also lasted with British Railways until September 1962. The loco behind is 'H' Class 0-4-4T No. 31533 (see photo above) - both are awaiting their final journey to the scrap yard.

Number	Class	W.Arrgt.	1948	1952	1955	1959	1963	1966	w/dwn	Notes
30058	M7	0-4-4T	YEO	71B	71B	71B	-	-	*09/60*	Push Pull fitted
30059	M7	0-4-4T	BM	71B	71B	71B	-	-	*02/61*	" " "
30060	M7	0-4-4T	GFD	71B	71B	71B	-	-	*07/61*	" " "
30061	USA	0-6-0T	SOT	71I	71I	71I	-	-	*11/62*	*Became DS233*
30062	USA	0-6-0T	SOT	71I	71I	71I	-	-	*11/62*	*Became DS234*
30063	USA	0-6-0T	SOT	71I	71I	71I	-	-	*05/62*	
30064	USA	0-6-0T	SOT	71I	71I	71I	71I	70D	*07/67*	
30065	USA	0-6-0T	SOT	71I	71I	71I	-	-	*10/62*	*Became DS237* Maunsell
30066	USA	0-6-0T	SOT	71I	71I	71I	-	-	*12/62*	*Became DS235*
30067	USA	0-6-0T	SOT	71I	71I	71I	71I	70D	*07/67*	
30068	USA	0-6-0T	SOT	71I	71I	71I	71I	-	*03/64*	
30069	USA	0-6-0T	SOT	71I	71I	71I	71I	70D	*07/67*	
30070	USA	0-6-0T	SOT	71I	71I	71I	-	-	*10/62*	*Became DS238* Wainwright
30071	USA	0-6-0T	SOT	71I	71I	71I	71I	70D	*07/67*	
30072	USA	0-6-0T	SOT	71I	71I	71I	70C	70C	*07/67*	
30073	USA	0-6-0T	SOT	71I	71I	71I	71I	70D	*01/67*	
30074	USA	0-6-0T	SOT	71I	71I	71I	71I	-	*03/63*	*Became DS236*
30081	B4	0-4-0T	SOT	-	-	-	-	-	*02/49*	*Was named* Jersey
30082	B4	0-4-0T	ELH	71A	71A	-	-	-	*07/57*	
30083	B4	0-4-0T	DOV	72D	71A	71A	-	-	*10/59*	
30084	B4	0-4-0T	PLY	74C	74C	73H	-	-	*08/59*	
30085	B4	0-4-0T	SOT	-	-	-	-	-	*02/49*	*Was named* Alderney
30086	B4	0-4-0T	BAT	71B	74C	70C	-	-	*02/59*	*Was named* Havre
30087	B4	0-4-0T	ELH	71B	71B	71B	-	-	*12/58*	
30088	B4	0-4-0T	ELH	71A	72D	71A	-	-	*07/59*	
30089	B4	0-4-0T	SOT	72D	72D	71A	70C	-	*03/63*	*Was named* Trouville
30090	B4	0-4-0T	BAT	-	-	-	-	-	*05/48*	*Was named* Caen
30091	B4	0-4-0T	PLY	-	-	-	-	-	*08/48*	
30092	B4	0-4-0T	BM	-	-	-	-	-	*04/49*	
30093	B4	0-4-0T	BM	71B	71B	71B	-	-	*04/60*	*Was named* St. Malo
30094	B4	0-4-0T	PLY	72D	72D	-	-	-	*03/57*	
30095	B4	0-4-0T	PLY	-	-	-	-	-	*04/49*	*Was named* Honfleur
30096	B4	0-4-0T	ELH	71A	71A	71A	71A	-	*10/63*	*Was named* Normandy
30097	B4	0-4-0T	SOT	-	-	-	-	-	*03/49*	*Was named* Brittany
30098	B4	0-4-0T	SOT	-	-	-	-	-	*02/49*	*Was named* Cherbourg
30099	B4	0-4-0T	BM	-	-	-	-	-	*02/49*	
30100	B4	0-4-0T	BM	-	-	-	-	-	*02/49*	
30101	B4	0-4-0T	SOT	-	-	-	-	-	*11/48*	*Was named* Dinan
30102	B4	0-4-0T	ELH	72D	72D	71A	71A	-	*09/63*	*Was named* Granville
30103	B4	0-4-0T	PLY	-	-	-	-	-	*04/49*	
30104	M7	0-4-4T	BM	71B	71B	71B	-	-	*05/61*	Push Pull fitted
30105	M7	0-4-4T	EXJ	71B	71B	71B	71B	-	*05/63*	" " "
30106	M7	0-4-4T	BM	71B	71B	71B	-	-	*11/60*	Push Pull fitted. Swapped identity with **30667** 02/61
30107	M7	0-4-4T	BM	71B	71B	71B	71B	-	*05/64*	Push Pull fitted
30108	M7	0-4-4T	GFD	70C	75D	71B	71B	-	*05/64*	" " "
30109	M7	0-4-4T	ELH	70C	70C	75A	-	-	*06/61*	" " "
30110	M7	0-4-4T	GFD	70C	70C	75A	71B	-	*05/63*	" " "
30111	M7	0-4-4T	BM	71B	71B	71B	71B	-	*01/64*	" " "
30112	M7	0-4-4T	BM	71B	71B	71B	-	-	*02/63*	
30113	T9	4-4-0	FRA	-	-	-	-	-	*05/51*	
30114	T9	4-4-0	FRA	-	-	-	-	-	*05/51*	
30115	T9	4-4-0	FRA	-	-	-	-	-	*05/51*	
30116	T9	4-4-0	PLY	-	-	-	-	-	*05/51*	
30117	T9	4-4-0	SAL	71C	71A	71A	-	-	*07/61*	
30118	T9	4-4-0	FRA	-	-	-	-	-	*05/51*	
30119	T9	4-4-0	9E	71C	-	-	-	-	*12/52*	
30120	T9	4-4-0	ELH	71C	71A	71A	-	-	*03/62*	Currently preserved as **S.R. 120**
30121	T9	4-4-0	ELH	-	-	-	-	-	*04/51*	
30122	T9	4-4-0	SAL	-	-	-	-	-	*04/51*	

Number	Class	W.Arrgt.	1948	1952	1955	1959	1963	1966	w/dwn	Notes
30123	M7	0-4-4T	9E	70A	70A	70A	-	-	06/59	
30124	M7	0-4-4T	EXJ	70A	70A	70C	-	-	05/61	
30125	M7	0-4-4T	ELH	71A	71A	71A	-	-	12/62	Push Pull fitted
30127	M7	0-4-4T	SAL	71A	71A	71B	71B	-	11/63	
30128	M7	0-4-4T	ELH	71B	71B	71B	-	-	01/60	Push Pull fitted. Swapped identity with 30031 01/60
30129	M7	0-4-4T	YEO	72C	75A	72C	72C	-	11/63	Push Pull fitted
30130	M7	0-4-4T	9E	70A	71A	70B	-	-	12/59	
30131	M7	0-4-4T	BM	72C	72C	72C	-	-	11/62	Push Pull fitted
30132	M7	0-4-4T	9E	70A	70A	70A	-	-	11/62	
30133	M7	0-4-4T	EXJ	72A	70A	70A	75F	-	03/64	Push Pull fitted
30134	L11	4-4-0	YEO	-	-	-	-	-	03/51	
30135	K10	4-4-0	EXJ	-	-	-	-	-	03/49	
30137	K10	4-4-0	EXJ	-	-	-	-	-	08/49	
30139	K10	4-4-0	FEL	-	-	-	-	-	09/48	
30140	K10	4-4-0	FEL	-	-	-	-	-	01/50	
30141	K10	4-4-0	GFD	-	-	-	-	-	10/49	
30142	K10	4-4-0	9E	-	-	-	-	-	01/50	
30143	K10	4-4-0	YEO	-	-	-	-	-	09/48	
30144	K10	4-4-0	FEL	-	-	-	-	-	07/49	
30145	K10	4-4-0	YEO	-	-	-	-	-	10/48	
30146	K10	4-4-0	DOR	-	-	-	-	-	02/48	
30147	B4	0-4-0T	SOT	-	-	-	-	-	02/49	Was named Dinard
30148	L11	4-4-0	ELH	-	-	-	-	-	03/52	
30150	K10	4-4-0	ELH	-	-	-	-	-	02/48	
30151	K10	4-4-0	ELH	-	-	-	-	-	02/50	
30152	K10	4-4-0	YEO	-	-	-	-	-	02/49	
30153	K10	4-4-0	FEL	-	-	-	-	-	03/49	
30154	L11	4-4-0	ELH	-	-	-	-	-	04/51	
30155	L11	4-4-0	ELH	-	-	-	-	-	04/51	
30156	L11	4-4-0	DOR	-	-	-	-	-	05/51	
30157	L11	4-4-0	ELH	-	-	-	-	-	03/52	
30158	L11	4-4-0	FEL	-	-	-	-	-	12/50	
30159	L11	4-4-0	ELH	-	-	-	-	-	03/51	
30160	G6	0-6-0T	9E	70E	70E	70D	-	-	04/59	
30161	L11	4-4-0	BM	-	-	-	-	-	02/50	
30162	G6	0-6-0T	DOR	71C	71B	-	-	-	03/58	
30163	L11	4-4-0	YEO	-	-	-	-	-	12/51	
30164	L11	4-4-0	FRA	-	-	-	-	-	10/51	
30165	L11	4-4-0	ELH	-	-	-	-	-	04/51	
30166	L11	4-4-0	FRA	-	-	-	-	-	07/50	
30167	L11	4-4-0	FEL	-	-	-	-	-	09/49	
30168	L11	4-4-0	BM	-	-	-	-	-	02/50	
30169	L11	4-4-0	BM	-	-	-	-	-	07/49	
30170	L11	4-4-0	FRA	-	-	-	-	-	06/52	
30171	L11	4-4-0	ELH	-	-	-	-	-	09/51	
30172	L11	4-4-0	FRA	-	-	-	-	-	06/52	
30173	L11	4-4-0	BM	-	-	-	-	-	05/51	
30174	L11	4-4-0	FEL	-	-	-	-	-	09/51	
30175	L11	4-4-0	ELH	-	-	-	-	-	12/51	
30176	B4	0-4-0T	SOT	-	-	-	-	-	06/48	Was named Guernsey
30177	O2	0-4-4T	DOR	71C	71A	70B	-	-	09/59	
30179	O2	0-4-4T	9E	71C	71A	70B	-	-	12/59	
30181	O2	0-4-4T	WAD	-	-	-	-	-	04/49	
30182	O2	0-4-4T	PLY	72D	72C	72A	-	-	01/60	
30183	O2	0-4-4T	PLY	72D	72D	83H	-	-	09/61	
30192	O2	0-4-4T	EXJ	72F	72D	83H	-	-	08/61	
30193	O2	0-4-4T	EXJ	72A	72A	83H	-	-	04/62	
30197	O2	0-4-4T	PLY	71C	-	-	-	-	02/53	
30198	O2	0-4-4T	ELH	-	-	-	-	-	04/49	

Number	Class	W.Arrgt.	1948	1952	1955	1959	1963	1966	w/dwn	Notes
30199	O2	0-4-4T	EXJ	72A	72A	72A	-	-	12/62	Not (?)
30200	O2	0-4-4T	ELH	72F	72F	72F	-	-	08/62	Not (?)
30203	O2	0-4-4T	WAD	72F	72F	-	-	-	12/55	
30204	O2	0-4-4T	9E	71B	-	-	-	-	02/53	
30207	O2	0-4-4T	EXJ	72D	70F	-	-	-	06/57	
30212	O2	0-4-4T	9E	71B	71B	71A	-	-	11/59	
30213	O2	0-4-4T	ELH	71A	-	-	-	-	02/53	
30216	O2	0-4-4T	PLY	72D	72D	-	-	-	11/57	
30221	O2	0-4-4T	DOR	70A	-	-	-	-	08/53	
30223	O2	0-4-4T	DOR	71B	71B	71A	-	-	10/61	
30224	O2	0-4-4T	EXJ	72A	70A	-	-	-	02/58	
30225	O2	0-4-4T	ELH	71A	72D	83H	-	-	12/62	
30229	O2	0-4-4T	DOR	71A	71A	71A	-	-	03/61	
30230	O2	0-4-4T	EXJ	70B	70B	-	-	-	08/56	
30231	O2	0-4-4T	ELH	71C	-	-	-	-	03/53	
30232	O2	0-4-4T	EXJ	72A	72A	72A	-	-	09/59	
30233	O2	0-4-4T	DOR	71A	71A	-	-	-	02/58	
30236	O2	0-4-4T	PLY	72D	72D	72F	-	-	01/60	
30237	G6	0-6-0T	SAL	-	-	-	-	-	03/49	
30238	G6	0-6-0T	YEO	70C	70C	70C	-	-	11/60	renumbered **DS682** 11/60
30239	G6	0-6-0T	BM	-	-	-	-	-	10/48	
30240	G6	0-6-0T	ELH	-	-	-	-	-	03/49	
30241	M7	0-4-4T	9E	70A	70A	70A	70E	-	07/63	
30242	M7	0-4-4T	ELH	70A	70A	-	-	-	06/58	
30243	M7	0-4-4T	SAL	70A	70A	-	-	-	09/58	
30244	M7	0-4-4T	9E	70A	70A	-	-	-	10/57	
30245	M7	0-4-4T	EXJ	72E	70A	70A	-	-	11/62	
30246	M7	0-4-4T	GFD	70C	70C	70C	-	-	10/61	
30247	M7	0-4-4T	BPL	72E	72E	72E	-	-	10/61	
30248	M7	0-4-4T	9E	70A	70A	70A	-	-	07/61	
30249	M7	0-4-4T	9E	70A	70A	70A	70E	-	07/63	
30250	M7	0-4-4T	BPL	72E	72E	-	-	-	08/57	
30251	M7	0-4-4T	BM	72E	72E	72E	70B	-	07/63	
30252	M7	0-4-4T	EXJ	72E	72E	72E	-	-	02/59	
30253	M7	0-4-4T	EXJ	72E	72E	72E	-	-	10/61	
30254	M7	0-4-4T	FEL	70B	72E	72E	71B	-	05/64	
30255	M7	0-4-4T	EXJ	72E	72E	72E	-	-	09/60	
30256	M7	0-4-4T	EXJ	72E	72E	72E	-	-	05/59	
30257	G6	0-6-0T	9E	-	-	-	-	-	02/49	
30258	G6	0-6-0T	RDG	70D	70D	70D	-	-	07/61	
30259	G6	0-6-0T	9E	-	-	-	-	-	12/50	
30260	G6	0-6-0T	RDG	71B	71B	71B	-	-	11/58	
30261	G6	0-6-0T	ELH	-	-	-	-	-	11/48	
30262	G6	0-6-0T	GFD	-	-	-	-	-	11/49	
30263	G6	0-6-0T	9E	-	-	-	-	-	09/49	
30264	G6	0-6-0T	ELH	-	-	-	-	-	02/49	
30265	G6	0-6-0T	BAS	-	-	-	-	-	08/49	
30266	G6	0-6-0T	9E	70D	72B	72B	-	-	06/60	
30267	G6	0-6-0T	ELH	-	-	-	-	-	02/49	
30268	G6	0-6-0T	GFD	-	-	-	-	-	12/50	
30269	G6	0-6-0T	GFD	-	-	-	-	-	10/49	
30270	G6	0-6-0T	GFD	70E	72B	72B	-	-	01/59	
30271	G6	0-6-0T	9E	-	-	-	-	-	09/48	
30272	G6	0-6-0T	ELH	-	-	-	-	-	06/50	renumbered **DS3152** 06/50
30273	G6	0-6-0T	9E	-	-	-	-	-	03/49	
30274	G6	0-6-0T	ELH	71H	71H	82G	-	-	10/60	
30275	G6	0-6-0T	ELH	-	-	-	-	-	12/49	
30276	G6	0-6-0T	YEO	-	-	-	-	-	10/49	
30277	G6	0-6-0T	ELH	70C	70C	70E	-	-	11/61	

Guildford based Class 'U' 2-6-0 No. 31639 lasted far longer than any other member of the class, not being withdrawn until June 1966. It is seen here hauling passenger stock and looking absolutely immaculate in B.R. mixed traffic lined black.

Number	Class	W.Arrgt.	1948	1952	1955	1959	1963	1966	w/dwn	Notes
30278	G6	0-6-0T	BAS	-	-	-	-	-	12/48	
30279	G6	0-6-0T	SAL	-	-	-	-	-	12/48	
30280	T9	4-4-0	FRA	-	-	-	-	-	05/51	
30281	T9	4-4-0	DOR	-	-	-	-	-	12/51	
30282	T9	4-4-0	EXJ	71A	-	-	-	-	03/54	
30283	T9	4-4-0	EXJ	71A	71A	-	-	-	12/57	
30284	T9	4-4-0	DOR	71A	71A	-	-	-	04/58	
30285	T9	4-4-0	SAL	71A	71A	-	-	-	06/58	
30286	T9	4-4-0	ELH	-	-	-	-	-	04/51	
30287	T9	4-4-0	FRA	71A	71A	71A	-	-	09/61	
30288	T9	4-4-0	SAL	71A	71A	71A	-	-	12/60	
30289	T9	4-4-0	PLY	71A	71A	71A	-	-	11/59	
30300	T9	4-4-0	DOR	71A	71A	71A	-	-	03/61	
30301	T9	4-4-0	EXJ	72B	72B	72B	-	-	08/59	
30302	T9	4-4-0	ELH	72B	-	-	-	-	10/52	
30303	T9	4-4-0	FRA	-	-	-	-	-	05/51	
30304	T9	4-4-0	FRA	72B	72B	-	-	-	09/57	
30305	T9	4-4-0	FRA	-	-	-	-	-	05/51	
30306	700	0-6-0	ELH	71A	71A	71A	-	-	04/62	
30307	T9	4-4-0	BAS	70C	-	-	-	-	12/52	
30308	700	0-6-0	GFD	70C	70C	70C	-	-	09/61	
30309	700	0-6-0	GFD	70C	72B	72B	-	-	12/62	
30310	T9	4-4-0	YEO	70C	71A	71B	-	-	05/59	
30311	T9	4-4-0	GFD	-	-	-	-	-	07/52	
30312	T9	4-4-0	SAL	-	-	-	-	-	03/52	
30313	T9	4-4-0	ELH	70C	72B	72B	-	-	07/61	
30314	T9	4-4-0	FRA	-	-	-	-	-	05/51	
30315	700	0-6-0	SAL	72B	72A	72B	-	-	12/62	
30316	700	0-6-0	ELH	71A	71A	71A	-	-	12/62	
30317	700	0-6-0	SAL	72B	72B	72A	-	-	07/61	
30318	M7	0-4-4T	BM	71B	71B	71B	-	-	12/59	
30319	M7	0-4-4T	9E	70A	70A	70A	-	-	01/60	
30320	M7	0-4-4T	EXJ	72A	70A	70A	-	-	02/63	
30321	M7	0-4-4T	BPL	72A	70A	70A	-	-	09/62	
30322	M7	0-4-4T	9E	70A	70A	70A	-	-	11/58	
30323	M7	0-4-4T	EXJ	72A	72A	72A	-	-	12/59	
30324	M7	0-4-4T	GFD	70C	70C	71B	-	-	09/59	
30325	700	0-6-0	GFD	70C	70C	70C	-	-	12/62	
30326	700	0-6-0	GFD	70C	70C	70C	-	-	02/62	
30327	700	0-6-0	GFD	70C	72B	72B	-	-	05/61	
30328	M7	0-4-4T	GFD	70C	70C	71A	75F	-	03/63	
30329	K10	4-4-0	EXJ	-	-	-	-	-	04/50	
30330	H15	4-6-0	SAL	72B	72B	-	-	-	05/57	
30331	H15	4-6-0	SAL	72B	72B	72B	-	-	03/61	
30332	H15	4-6-0	SAL	72B	72B	-	-	-	11/56	
30333	H15	4-6-0	SAL	72B	72B	72B	-	-	10/58	
30334	H15	4-6-0	SAL	72B	72B	-	-	-	06/58	
30335	H15	4-6-0	SAL	72B	72B	72B	-	-	06/59	
30336	T9	4-4-0	ELH	70C	-	-	-	-	02/53	
30337	T9	4-4-0	BM	70C	70C	70C	-	-	11/58	
30338	T9	4-4-0	FRA	70C	70A	70A	-	-	04/61	
30339	700	0-6-0	9E	70B	70B	70B	-	-	05/62	
30340	K10	4-4-0	YEO	-	-	-	-	-	06/48	
30341	K10	4-4-0	ELH	-	-	-	-	-	12/49	
30343	K10	4-4-0	GFD	-	-	-	-	-	02/48	

Number	Class	W.Arrgt	1948	1952	1955	1959	1963	1966	w/dwn	Notes
30345	K10	4-4-0	ELH	-	-	-	-	-	09/49	
30346	700	0-6-0	GFD	70B	70B	70B	-	-	11/62	
30348	G6	0-6-0T	BAS	-	-	-	-	-	08/48	
30349	G6	0-6-0T	GFD	70C	70C	70C	-	-	07/61	
30350	700	0-6-0	ELH	71A	70C	70C	-	-	03/62	
30351	G6	0-6-0T	ELH	-	-	-	-	-	03/49	
30352	700	0-6-0	GFD	70B	70B	70B	-	-	06/59	
30353	G6	0-6-0T	9E	-	-	-	-	-	03/51	
30354	G6	0-6-0T	9E	-	-	-	-	-	11/49	
30355	700	0-6-0	SAL	70B	70B	70B	-	-	02/61	
30356	M7	0-4-4T	EXJ	72A	70F	70F	-	-	12/58	
30357	M7	0-4-4T	ELH	72A	70F	70F	-	-	04/61	
30361	T1	0-4-4T	SAL	-	-	-	-	-	02/49	
30363	T1	0-4-4T	BM	-	-	-	-	-	06/48	
30366	T1	0-4-4T	ELH	-	-	-	-	-	10/48	
30367	T1	0-4-4T	ELH	-	-	-	-	-	06/51	
30368	700	0-6-0	BAS	70D	70D	70D	-	-	12/62	
30374	M7	0-4-4T	EXJ	72A	72A	72A	-	-	10/59	
30375	M7	0-4-4T	EXJ	72A	71A	71A	-	-	09/62	
30376	M7	0-4-4T	EXJ	72A	71A	71A	-	-	01/59	
30377	M7	0-4-4T	EXJ	72A	71A	71A	-	-	08/62	
30378	M7	0-4-4T	GFD	71A	71A	71A	-	-	12/62	
30379	M7	0-4-4T	BM	71A	71A	71A	75F	-	10/63	
30380	K10	4-4-0	9E	-	-	-	-	-	06/49	
30382	K10	4-4-0	SAL	-	-	-	-	-	08/50	
30383	K10	4-4-0	FEL	-	-	-	-	-	05/49	
30384	K10	4-4-0	FRA	-	-	-	-	-	06/51	
30385	K10	4-4-0	FEL	-	-	-	-	-	02/49	
30386	K10	4-4-0	9E	-	-	-	-	-	08/49	
30389	K10	4-4-0	SAL	-	-	-	-	-	07/51	
30390	K10	4-4-0	9E	-	-	-	-	-	11/50	
30391	K10	4-4-0	9E	-	-	-	-	-	10/49	
30392	K10	4-4-0	9E	-	-	-	-	-	10/48	
30393	K10	4-4-0	ELH	-	-	-	-	-	02/49	
30394	K10	4-4-0	ELH	-	-	-	-	-	05/49	
30395	S11	4-4-0	ELH	-	-	-	-	-	10/51	
30396	S11	4-4-0	FRA	-	-	-	-	-	11/51	
30397	S11	4-4-0	ELH	-	-	-	-	-	12/51	
30398	S11	4-4-0	BM	-	-	-	-	-	12/51	
30399	S11	4-4-0	BM	-	-	-	-	-	12/51	
30400	S11	4-4-0	FRA	71C	-	-	-	-	11/54	
30401	S11	4-4-0	FRA	-	-	-	-	-	09/51	
30402	S11	4-4-0	FRA	-	-	-	-	-	03/51	
30403	S11	4-4-0	FRA	-	-	-	-	-	10/51	
30404	S11	4-4-0	FRA	-	-	-	-	-	10/51	
30405	L11	4-4-0	SAL	-	-	-	-	-	02/51	
30406	L11	4-4-0	9E	-	-	-	-	-	06/51	
30407	L11	4-4-0	BAS	-	-	-	-	-	11/50	
30408	L11	4-4-0	EXJ	-	-	-	-	-	03/51	
30409	L11	4-4-0	EXJ	-	-	-	-	-	06/51	
30410	L11	4-4-0	DOR	-	-	-	-	-	12/49	
30411	L11	4-4-0	ELH	-	-	-	-	-	06/52	
30412	L11	4-4-0	YEO	-	-	-	-	-	12/50	
30413	L11	4-4-0	FRA	-	-	-	-	-	03/51	
30414	L11	4-4-0	FRA	-	-	-	-	-	05/51	
30415	L12	4-4-0	BM	71D	-	-	-	-	02/53	
30416	L12	4-4-0	GFD	-	-	-	-	-	06/51	
30417	L12	4-4-0	FRA	-	-	-	-	-	12/51	
30418	L12	4-4-0	BAS	-	-	-	-	-	06/51	

Number	Class	W.Arrgt.	1948	1952	1955	1959	1963	1966	w/dwn	Notes
30419	L12	4-4-0	GFD	-	-	-	-	-	12/51	
30420	L12	4-4-0	ELH	-	-	-	-	-	09/51	
30421	L12	4-4-0	SAL	-	-	-	-	-	09/51	
30422	L12	4-4-0	ELH	-	-	-	-	-	09/51	
30423	L12	4-4-0	ELH	-	-	-	-	-	07/51	
30424	L12	4-4-0	FRA	-	-	-	-	-	07/51	
30425	L12	4-4-0	FRA	-	-	-	-	-	09/51	
30426	L12	4-4-0	BAS	-	-	-	-	-	11/51	
30427	L12	4-4-0	9E	-	-	-	-	-	11/51	
30428	L12	4-4-0	ELH	-	-	-	-	-	04/51	
30429	L12	4-4-0	BM	-	-	-	-	-	10/51	
30430	L12	4-4-0	ELH	-	-	-	-	-	03/51	
30431	L12	4-4-0	9E	-	-	-	-	-	10/51	
30432	L12	4-4-0	SAL	-	-	-	-	-	10/51	
30433	L12	4-4-0	GFD	-	-	-	-	-	12/51	
30434	L12	4-4-0	GFD	70C	70C	-	-	-	03/55	
30435	L11	4-4-0	9E	-	-	-	-	-	12/49	
30436	L11	4-4-0	EXJ	-	-	-	-	-	07/51	
30437	L11	4-4-0	ELH	-	-	-	-	-	06/52	
30438	L11	4-4-0	GFD	-	-	-	-	-	10/51	
30439	L11	4-4-0	EXJ	-	-	-	-	-	05/49	
30440	L11	4-4-0	9E	-	-	-	-	-	05/49	
30441	L11	4-4-0	FRA	-	-	-	-	-	04/51	
30442	L11	4-4-0	9E	-	-	-	-	-	12/51	
30443	T14	4-4-0	9E	-	-	-	-	-	05/49	
30444	T14	4-4-0	9E	-	-	-	-	-	02/50	
30445	T14	4-4-0	9E	-	-	-	-	-	11/48	
30446	T14	4-4-0	9E	-	-	-	-	-	05/51	
30447	T14	4-4-0	9E	-	-	-	-	-	12/49	

Number & Name		Class	W. A.	1948	1952	1955	1959	w/dwn	Notes
30448	Sir Tristram	N15	4-6-0	SAL	72B	72B	72B	08/60	
30449	Sir Torre	"	"	SAL	72B	72B	72B	12/59	
30450	Sir Kay	"	"	SAL	72B	72B	72B	09/60	
30451	Sir Lamorak	"	"	SAL	72B	72B	72B	06/62	
30452	Sir Meliagrance	"	"	SAL	72B	72B	72B	08/59	
30453	King Arthur	"	"	SAL	72B	72B	72B	07/61	
30454	Queen Guinevere	"	"	SAL	72B	72B	72B	10/58	
30455	Sir Launcelot	"	"	SAL	70A	70A	70D	04/59	
30456	Sir Galahad	"	"	SAL	70A	70A	70D	05/60	
30457	Sir Bedivere	"	"	SAL	70A	70A	70A	05/61	
30458	Ironside	0458	0-4-0ST	GFD	70C	-	-	06/54	formerly S.R. 3458

Number	Class	W.Arrgt.	1948	1952	1955	1959	1963	1966	w/dwn	Notes
30459	T14	4-6-0	9E	-	-	-	-	-	11/48	
30460	T14	4-6-0	9E	-	-	-	-	-	11/48	
30461	T14	4-6-0	9E	-	-	-	-	-	06/51	
30462	T14	4-6-0	9E	-	-	-	-	-	02/50	
30463	D15	4-4-0	ELH	-	-	-	-	-	12/51	
30464	D15	4-4-0	ELH	71A	-	-	-	-	11/54	
30465	D15	4-4-0	ELH	71A	70A	-	-	-	01/56	
30466	D15	4-4-0	ELH	71A	-	-	-	-	10/52	
30467	D15	4-4-0	ELH	71A	70A	-	-	-	09/55	
30468	D15	4-4-0	ELH	-	-	-	-	-	03/52	
30469	D15	4-4-0	ELH	-	-	-	-	-	12/51	
30470	D15	4-4-0	ELH	71A	-	-	-	-	12/52	
30471	D15	4-4-0	ELH	71A	-	-	-	-	03/54	
30472	D15	4-4-0	ELH	-	-	-	-	-	03/52	
30473	D15	4-4-0	ELH	71A	71A	71A	-	-	07/59	

Number	Class	W.Arrgt.	1948	1952	1955	1959	1963	1966	w/dwn	Notes
30474	H15	4-6-0	ELH	71A	71A	71A	-	-	04/60	
30475	H15	4-6-0	SAL	71A	71A	71A	-	-	12/61	
30476	H15	4-6-0	SAL	71A	71A	71A	-	-	12/61	
30477	H15	4-6-0	9E	71A	71A	71A	-	-	07/59	
30478	H15	4-6-0	ELH	71A	71A	70A	-	-	04/59	
30479	M7	0-4-4T	ELH	71A	71A	71A	-	-	04/61	
30480	M7	0-4-4T	FRA	71A	71A	71A	71B	-	05/64	
30481	M7	0-4-4T	GFD	71A	71A	71A	-	-	05/59	
30482	H15	4-6-0	9E	70A	70A	70A	-	-	05/59	
30483	H15	4-6-0	9E	70A	70A	-	-	-	06/57	
30484	H15	4-6-0	9E	70A	70A	70A	-	-	05/59	
30485	H15	4-6-0	9E	70A	70A	-	-	-	04/55	
30486	H15	4-6-0	9E	70A	70A	70A	-	-	07/59	
30487	H15	4-6-0	9E	70A	70A	-	-	-	11/57	
30488	H15	4-6-0	9E	70A	70A	70A	-	-	04/59	
30489	H15	4-6-0	9E	70A	70A	70A	-	-	01/61	
30490	H15	4-6-0	9E	70A	70A	-	-	-	07/55	
30491	H15	4-6-0	9E	70A	70A	70A	-	-	01/61	
30492	G16	4-8-0T	FEL	70B	70B	70B	-	-	02/59	
30493	G16	4-8-0T	FEL	70B	70B	70B	-	-	12/59	
30494	G16	4-8-0T	FEL	70B	70B	70B	-	-	12/62	
30495	G16	4-8-0T	FEL	70B	70B	70B	-	-	12/62	
30496	S15	4-6-0	FEL	70B	70B	70B	70B	-	06/63	
30497	S15	4-6-0	FEL	70B	70B	70B	70B	-	07/63	
30498	S15	4-6-0	FEL	70B	70B	70B	70B	-	06/63	
30499	S15	4-6-0	FEL	70B	70B	70B	70B	-	01/64	
30500	S15	4-6-0	FEL	70B	70B	70B	70B	-	06/63	
30501	S15	4-6-0	FEL	70B	70B	70B	70B	-	06/63	
30502	S15	4-6-0	FEL	70B	70B	70B	-	-	11/62	
30503	S15	4-6-0	FEL	70B	70B	70B	70B	-	06/63	
30504	S15	4-6-0	FEL	70B	70B	70B	-	-	11/62	
30505	S15	4-6-0	FEL	70B	70B	70B	-	-	11/62	
30506	S15	4-6-0	FEL	70B	70B	70B	70B	-	01/64	
30507	S15	4-6-0	FEL	70B	70B	70B	70B	-	12/63	
30508	S15	4-6-0	FEL	70B	70B	70B	70B	-	12/63	
30509	S15	4-6-0	FEL	70B	70B	70B	70B	-	07/63	
30510	S15	4-6-0	FEL	70B	70B	70B	70B	-	06/63	
30511	S15	4-6-0	FEL	70B	70B	70B	70B	-	07/63	
30512	S15	4-6-0	FEL	70B	70B	70B	70B	-	03/64	
30513	S15	4-6-0	FEL	70B	70B	70B	70B	-	03/63	
30514	S15	4-6-0	FEL	70B	70B	70B	70B	-	07/63	
30515	S15	4-6-0	FEL	70B	70B	70B	70B	-	07/63	
30516	H16	4-6-2T	FEL	70B	70B	70B	-	-	11/62	
30517	H16	4-6-2T	FEL	70B	70B	70B	-	-	11/62	
30518	H16	4-6-2T	FEL	70B	70B	70B	-	-	11/62	
30519	H16	4-6-2T	FEL	70B	70B	70B	-	-	11/62	
30520	H16	4-6-2T	FEL	70B	70B	70B	-	-	11/62	
30521	H15	4-6-0	ELH	70A	70A	70A	-	-	12/61	
30522	H15	4-6-0	ELH	70A	70A	70A	-	-	10/61	
30523	H15	4-6-0	ELH	70A	70A	70A	-	-	09/61	
30524	H15	4-6-0	ELH	70A	70A	70A	-	-	02/61	
30530	Q	0-6-0	ELH	71A	71A	71A	72A	-	12/64	
30531	Q	0-6-0	TWW	71A	71A	71A	72A	-	07/64	
30532	Q	0-6-0	ELH	71A	71A	71A	70E	-	01/64	
30533	Q	0-6-0	RED	75C	75C	75C	71B	-	03/63	
30534	Q	0-6-0	TWW	75C	75C	75C	-	-	12/62	
30535	Q	0-6-0	ELH	71A	71A	71A	71B	-	04/65	
30536	Q	0-6-0	ELH	71A	71A	71A	75E	-	01/64	
30537	Q	0-6-0	RED	75C	75C	75C	-	-	12/62	

Number	Class	W.Arrgt.	1948	1952	1955	1959	1963	w/dwn	Notes
30538	Q	0-6-0	RED	75C	75C	75C	71B	07/63	
30539	Q	0-6-0	RED	75C	75C	71B	71B	01/63	
30540	Q	0-6-0	HOR	75E	75C	75C	-	11/62	
30541	Q	0-6-0	3B	75E	71B	71B	70D	11/64	
30542	Q	0-6-0	3B	71A	71A	71A	70C	12/64	
30543	Q	0-6-0	HOR	71A	71A	71A	75E	12/64	
30544	Q	0-6-0	HOR	75E	75D	75D	75E	01/64	
30545	Q	0-6-0	RED	75D	75D	75D	75E	04/65	
30546	Q	0-6-0	RED	75D	75D	75D	75E	05/64	
30547	Q	0-6-0	RED	75C	75C	75D	75E	01/64	
30548	Q	0-6-0	BM	71B	71B	71B	71A	03/65	
30549	Q	0-6-0	BM	71B	71B	75C	75E	07/63	
30564	0395	0-6-0	EXJ	72A	72A	-	-	04/58	formerly S.R. 3029
30565	0395	0-6-0	GFD	71A	-	-	-	02/53	formerly S.R. 3083
30566	0395	0-6-0	ELH	71A	71A	71A	-	02/59	formerly S.R. 3101
30567	0395	0-6-0	FEL	70B	70B	70B	-	09/59	formerly S.R. 3154
30568	0395	0-6-0	GFD	70B	70B	-	-	04/58	formerly S.R. 3155
30569	0395	0-6-0	FEL	70B	70B	-	-	06/56	formerly S.R. 3163
30570	0395	0-6-0	FEL	70B	70B	-	-	12/56	formerly S.R. 3167
30571	0395	0-6-0	ELH	70B	-	-	-	07/53	formerly S.R. 3397
30572	0395	0-6-0	FEL	70B	70B	-	-	01/57	formerly S.R. 3400
30573	0395	0-6-0	FEL	70B	70B	-	-	11/56	formerly S.R. 3433
30574	0395	0-6-0	GFD	70C	70C	-	-	01/57	formerly S.R. 3436
30575	0395	0-6-0	GFD	70C	70C	-	-	12/58	formerly S.R. 3439
30576	0395	0-6-0	KESR	-	-	-	-	12/50	formerly S.R. 3440. O/l to KESR
30577	0395	0-6-0	SAL	72C	70C	-	-	02/56	formerly S.R. 3441
30578	0395	0-6-0	GFD	70C	70C	-	-	08/57	formerly S.R. 3442
30579	0395	0-6-0	FEL	70C	70C	-	-	01/56	formerly S.R. 3496
30580	0395	0-6-0	GFD	72A	70C	-	-	06/57	formerly S.R. 3506
30581	0395	0-6-0	ELH	72A	-	-	-	03/53	formerly S.R. 3509
30582	0415	4-4-2T	EXJ	72A	72A	72A	-	07/61	formerly S.R. 3125
30583	0415	4-4-2T	EXJ	72A	72A	72A	-	07/61	formerly S.R. 3488
30584	0415	4-4-2T	EXJ	72A	72A	72A	-	02/61	formerly S.R. 3520
30585	0298	2-4-0WT	WAD	72F	72F	72F	-	12/62	formerly S.R. 3314
30586	0298	2-4-0WT	WAD	72F	72F	72F	-	12/62	formerly S.R. 3329
30587	0298	2-4-0WT	WAD	72F	72F	72F	-	12/62	formerly S.R. 3298
30588	C14	0-4-0T	ELH	71A	71A	-	-	12/57	formerly S.R. 3741
30589	C14	0-4-0T	ELH	71A	71A	-	-	06/57	formerly S.R. 3744
30618	A12	0-4-2	GFD	-	-	-	-	02/48	
30627	A12	0-4-2	ELH	-	-	-	-	12/48	
30629	A12	0-4-2	ELH	-	-	-	-	12/48	
30636	A12	0-4-2	ELH	-	-	-	-	10/48	
30667	M7	0-4-4T	9E	72A	72A	72A	72A	05/64	swapped identity with 30106 02/61
30668	M7	0-4-4T	EXJ	72A	72A	72A	-	09/61	
30669	M7	0-4-4T	EXJ	72A	72A	-	-	07/61	
30670	M7	0-4-4T	BPL	72A	72A	72A	72E	03/63	
30671	M7	0-4-4T	EXJ	72A	72A	72E	-	07/59	
30672	M7	0-4-4T	9E	-	-	-	-	05/48	

Companion volumes :

Part 1 : Western Region, Nos. 1 - 9799.
Part 3 : London Midland & Scottish Regions, Nos. 40000 - 58937
Part 4 : Eastern, North Eastern & Scottish Regions, Nos. 60001 - 69999
Part 5 : B.R. Standard and 'Austerity' Locomotives, Nos. 70000 - 92250
Part 6 : B.R. Diesel & Electric Locomotives (1948 - 1968)

Available direct from the Publisher or from Transport Bookshops everywhere.

Although British Railways' mixed traffic livery looked good on nearly every loco to which it was applied, it sits very uncomfortably on ex - S.E.C.R. Class 'L' 4-4-0 No. 31176.

Number	Class	W.Arrgt.	1948	1952	1955	1959	1963	1966	w/dwn	Notes
30673	M7	0-4-4T	9E	72B	72B	72B	-	-	08/60	
39674	M7	0-4-4T	ELH	72B	72B	72B	-	-	08/61	
30675	M7	0-4-4T	SAL	72B	70C	-	-	-	03/58	
30676	M7	0-4-4T	9E	72A	72A	72A	-	-	07/61	
30687	700	0-6-0	FEL	70B	70B	70B	-	-	09/60	
30688	700	0-6-0	FEL	70B	70B	-	-	-	09/57	
30689	700	0-6-0	FEL	70B	70B	70B			11/62	
30690	700	0-6-0	SAL	72B	71B	71B	-	-	12/62	
30691	700	0-6-0	SAL	72B	72A	72A	-	-	07/61	
30692	700	0-6-0	9E	70A	70A	70A	-	-	01/62	
30693	700	0-6-0	BAS	70C	70C	70C	-	-	07/61	
30694	700	0-6-0	9E	70A	70A	70A	-	-	06/61	
30695	700	0-6-0	DOR	71B	71B	71B	-	-	12/62	
30696	700	0-6-0	BM	70B	70B	70B	-	-	08/61	
30697	700	0-6-0	FEL	70B	70A	70C	-	-	11/62	
30698	700	0-6-0	FEL	70B	70A	70C	-	-	05/62	
30699	700	0-6-0	9E	70A	70A	70A	-	-	07/61	
30700	700	0-6-0	BM	70A	70A	70D	-	-	11/62	
30701	700	0-6-0	9E	70A	70A	70A	-	-	07/61	
30702	T9	4-4-0	YEO	72B	72B	72B	-	-	10/59	
30703	T9	4-4-0	WAD	72B	-	-	-	-	10/52	
30704	T9	4-4-0	GFD	-	-	-	-	-	10/51	
30705	T9	4-4-0	ELH	70D	70D	-	-	-	01/58	
30706	T9	4-4-0	BAS	72C	71B	71B	-	-	05/59	
30707	T9	4-4-0	ELH	70D	72C	71B	-	-	03/61	
30708	T9	4-4-0	BAS	70D	72A	-	-	-	12/57	
30709	T9	4-4-0	SAL	72A	72A	72A	-	-	07/61	
30710	T9	4-4-0	YEO	72A	72A	72A	-	-	03/59	
30711	T9	4-4-0	PLY	72A	72A	72A	-	-	08/59	
30712	T9	4-4-0	YEO	72A	72A	72A	-	-	11/58	
30713	T9	4-4-0	ELH	-	-	-	-	-	04/51	
30714	T9	4-4-0	YEO	-	-	-	-	-	04/51	
30715	T9	4-4-0	SAL	72A	72A	72A	-	-	07/61	
30716	T9	4-4-0	YEO	-	-	-	-	-	10/51	
30717	T9	4-4-0	WAD	72E	72A	72A	-	-	07/61	
30718	T9	4-4-0	9E	70A	70A	70A	-	-	03/61	
30719	T9	4-4-0	BM	70A	70A	70A	-	-	03/61	
30721	T9	4-4-0	SAL	70A	72B	-	-	-	01/58	
30722	T9	4-4-0	ELH	-	-	-	-	-	04/51	
30723	T9	4-4-0	EXJ	-	-	-	-	-	06/51	
30724	T9	4-4-0	EXJ	70A	70D	70D	-	-	05/59	
30725	T9	4-4-0	EXJ	71D	-	-	-	-	12/52	
30726	T9	4-4-0	GFD	71D	70F	72A	-	-	08/59	
30727	T9	4-4-0	SAL	71B	72A	-	-	-	09/58	
30728	T9	4-4-0	BM	71B	71B	-	-	-	10/56	
30729	T9	4-4-0	SAL	71B	70F	72B	-	-	03/61	
30730	T9	4-4-0	EXJ	71D	70F	-	-	-	08/57	
30731	T9	4-4-0	FRA	-	-	-	-	-	05/51	
30732	T9	4-4-0	FRA	71D	70F	70F	-	-	10/59	
30733	T9	4-4-0	FRA	-	-	-	-	-	06/52	

Number & Name		Class	W. A.	1948	1952	1955	1959	1963	1966	w/dwn	Notes
30736	Excalibur	N15	4-6-0	BM	71B	71B	-	-	-	10/56	
30737	King Uther	"	"	ELH	71B	71B	-	-	-	08/56	
30738	King Pellinore	"	"	9E	71B	71B	-	-	-	03/58	
30739	King Leodegrance	"	"	ELH	71B	71B	-	-	-	05/57	
30740	Merlin	"	"	ELH	71B	71B	-	-	-	12/55	
30741	Joyous Gard	"	"	ELH	71B	71B	-	-	-	02/56	
30742	Camelot	"	"	9E	71B	71B	-	-	-	02/57	

Class N1 2-6-0 No. 31878, always a Hither Green engine in B.R. days, clearly shows the beefy outside cylinders and deep front bufferbeam which distinguished this class from the two cylindered 'N' class from which they were derived. There were only six 'N1's compared to eighty class 'N's.

Class O1 0-6-0 No. 31064, seems to be blowing off steam in this photo. The body mounted springs on the tender make the loco look older than it really is. No. 31064 was withdrawn during May 1958 from Ashford M.P.D.

Number & Name		Class	W. A.	1948	1952	1955	1959	1963	1966	w/dwn	Notes
30743	Lyonnesse	N15	4-6-0	BM	71B	71B	-	-	-	10/55	
30744	Maid of Astolat	N15	4-6-0	SAL	70A	70A	-	-	-	01/56	
30745	Tintagel	N15	4-6-0	ELH	70D	70D	-	-	-	02/56	
30746	Pendragon	N15	4-6-0	SAL	71A	71A	-	-	-	11/55	
30747	Elaine	N15	4-6-0	EXJ	71A	71A	-	-	-	10/56	
30748	Vivien	N15	4-6-0	ELH	71A	71A	-	-	-	09/57	
30749	Iseult	N15	4-6-0	ELH	71A	70D	-	-	-	06/57	
30750	Morgan le Fay	N15	4-6-0	ELH	70A	70A	-	-	-	07/57	
30751	Etarre	N15	4-6-0	ELH	70A	70A	-	-	-	06/57	
30752	Linette	N15	4-6-0	ELH	70A	70A	-	-	-	12/55	
30753	Melisande	N15	4-6-0	9E	70D	70D	-	-	-	03/57	
30754	The Green Knight	N15	4-6-0	ELH	70D	-	-	-	-	02/53	
30755	The Red Knight	N15	4-6-0	ELH	70A	70A	-	-	-	05/57	
30756	A. S. Harris	756	0-6-0T	ELH	-	-	-	-	-	11/51	
30757	Earl of Mount Edgcumbe	757	0-6-2T	PLY	72D	72D	-	-	-	12/57	
30758	Lord St. Levan	757	0-6-2T	PLY	72D	72D	-	-	-	12/56	
30763	Sir Bors de Ganis	N15	4-6-0	BAT	73A	73A	70A	-	-	09/60	
30764	Sir Gawain	N15	4-6-0	BAT	73A	73A	71B	-	-	07/61	
30765	Sir Gareth	N15	4-6-0	BAT	73A	73A	70D	-	-	09/62	
30766	Sir Geraint	N15	4-6-0	9E	73A	73A	73A	-	-	12/58	
30767	Sir Valence	N15	4-6-0	DOV	73A	73A	73A	-	-	06/59	
30768	Sir Balin	N15	4-6-0	DOV	73A	73A	73A	-	-	10/61	
30769	Sir Balan	N15	4-6-0	DOV	73A	73A	73A	-	-	02/60	
30770	Sir Prianius	N15	4-6-0	DOV	74C	73A	71A	-	-	11/62	
30771	Sir Sagramore	N15	4-6-0	DOV	73A	73A	71B	-	-	03/61	
30772	Sir Percivale	N15	4-6-0	BM	74C	73C	71B	-	-	09/61	
30773	Sir Lavaine	N15	4-6-0	9E	74C	73A	70D	-	-	02/62	
30774	Sir Gaheris	N15	4-6-0	9E	73A	73A	70A	-	-	01/60	
30775	Sir Agravaine	N15	4-6-0	BAT	74C	74C	73H	-	-	02/60	
30776	Sir Galagars	N15	4-6-0	BAT	74C	74C	73H	-	-	01/59	
30777	Sir Lamiel	N15	4-6-0	ELH	74C	74C	73H	-	-	10/61	
30778	Sir Pelleas	N15	4-6-0	BAT	74C	70A	70A	-	-	05/59	
30779	Sir Colgrevance	N15	4-6-0	9E	74C	70A	70A	-	-	07/59	
30780	Sir Persant	N15	4-6-0	BAT	70A	70A	71B	-	-	07/59	
30781	Sir Aglovale	N15	4-6-0	BAT	71A	70A	71B	-	-	05/62	
30782	Sir Brian	N15	4-6-0	9E	71B	71B	71B	-	-	09/62	
30783	Sir Gillemere	N15	4-6-0	9E	71B	71B	71B	-	-	02/61	
30784	Sir Nerovens	N15	4-6-0	ELH	71A	71A	71A	-	-	10/59	
30785	Sir Mador de la Porte	N15	4-6-0	ELH	71A	71A	71A	-	-	10/59	
30786	Sir Lionel	N15	4-6-0	9E	71A	71A	71A	-	-	08/59	
30787	Sir Menadeuke	N15	4-6-0	BM	71A	71A	71A	-	-	02/59	
30788	Sir Urre of the Mount	N15	4-6-0	9E	71A	71A	71A	-	-	02/62	
30789	Sir Guy	N15	4-6-0	BM	71A	71A	71A	-	-	12/59	
30790	Sir Villiars	N15	4-6-0	BM	71A	71A	71A	-	-	10/61	
30791	Sir Uwaine	N15	4-6-0	9E	73A	73A	71A	-	-	05/60	
30792	Sir Hervis de Revel	N15	4-6-0	9E	73A	73A	71A	-	-	02/59	
30793	Sir Ontzlake	N15	4-6-0	BAT	73A	73A	73A	-	-	08/62	
30794	Sir Ector de Maris	N15	4-6-0	BAT	73A	73A	73A	-	-	08/60	
30795	Sir Dinadan	N15	4-6-0	BAT	73A	73A	73A	-	-	07/62	
30796	Sir Dodinas le Savage	N15	4-6-0	BAT	74C	74C	73C	-	-	02/62	
30797	Sir Blamor de Ganis	N15	4-6-0	BAT	74C	74C	73H	-	-	06/59	
30798	Sir Hectimere	N15	4-6-0	BA	74C	74C	73H	-	-	06/62	
30799	Sir Ironside	N15	4-6-0	BA	73B	73B	73B	-	-	02/61	
30800	Sir Meleaus de Lile	N15	4-6-0	HIT	73B	73B	73B	-	-	08/61	
30801	Sir Meliot de Logres	N15	4-6-0	AFD	73B	73B	73B	-	-	04/59	
30802	Sir Durnore	N15	4-6-0	AFD	74A	74A	73A	-	-	07/61	
30803	Sir Harry le Fise Lake	N15	4-6-0	AFD	74A	74A	73A	-	-	08/61	
30804	Sir Cador of Cornwall	N15	4-6-0	AFD	74A	74A	73H	-	-	02/62	
30805	Sir Constantine	N15	4-6-0	AFD	74A	74A	73H	-	-	11/59	
30806	Sir Galleron	N15	4-6-0	AFD	73C	73C	73C	-	-	04/61	

*Class E4 No. 32517, one of the ubiquitous 0-6-2Ts built for the London Brighton &
South Coast Railway. The L.B.S.C.R. preferred the 0-6-2T wheel arrangement to the
0-4-4Ts used by the S.E.C.R. & L.S.W.R. for similar duties.*

*Class C2X No. 32552 looks top heavy as it awaits its next duty.   The L.B.S.C.R. were
fond of putting larger boilers onto their engines, sometimes with disastrous aesthetic
results.   No. 32552 was withdrawn from Bricklayers Arms (73B) during June 1961.*

Number	Class	W.Arrgt.	1948	1952	1955	1959	1963	1966	w/dwn	Notes
30823	S15	4-6-0	EXJ	72B	72B	72B	70E	-	11/64	
30824	S15	4-6-0	EXJ	72B	72B	72B	70E	-	09/65	
30825	S15	4-6-0	EXJ	72B	72B	72B	70E	-	01/64	
30826	S15	4-6-0	EXJ	72B	72B	72B	-	-	11/62	
30827	S15	4-6-0	EXJ	72B	72B	72B	70E	-	01/64	
30828	S15	4-6-0	SAL	72B	72B	72B	70E	-	01/64	
30829	S15	4-6-0	SAL	72B	72B	72B	70E	-	11/63	
30830	S15	4-6-0	SAL	72B	72B	72B	70E	-	07/64	
30831	S15	4-6-0	SAL	72B	72B	72B	70E	-	11/63	
30832	S15	4-6-0	SAL	72B	72B	72B	70E	-	01/64	
30833	S15	4-6-0	FEL	70B	70B	70B	70B	-	05/65	
30834	S15	4-6-0	FEL	70B	70B	70B	70B	-	11/64	
30835	S15	4-6-0	FEL	75B	75B	75B	75B	-	11/64	
30836	S15	4-6-0	FEL	75B	75B	75B	75B	-	06/64	
30837	S15	4-6-0	FEL	75B	75B	75B	70B	-	09/65	
30838	S15	4-6-0	FEL	70B	70B	70B	70B	-	09/65	
30839	S15	4-6-0	FEL	70B	70B	70B	70B	-	09/65	
30840	S15	4-6-0	FEL	70B	70B	70B	70B	-	09/64	
30841	S15	4-6-0	FEL	72A	72A	72A	72A	-	01/64	
30842	S15	4-6-0	FEL	72A	72A	72A	72A	-	09/65	
30843	S15	4-6-0	EXJ	72A	72A	72A	72A	-	09/64	
30844	S15	4-6-0	EXJ	72A	72A	72A	72A	-	06/64	
30845	S15	4-6-0	EXJ	72A	72A	72A	72A	-	07/63	
30846	S15	4-6-0	EXJ	72B	72A	72A	-	-	01/63	
30847	S15	4-6-0	EXJ	72B	72B	72B	75B	-	01/64	

Number & Name		Class	W. A.	1948	1952	1955	1959	1963	w/dwn	Notes
30850	Lord Nelson	LN	4-6-0	BM	71A	71A	71A	-	08/62	
30851	Sir Francis Drake	"	"	BM	71A	71A	71A	-	12/61	
30852	Sir Walter Raleigh	"	"	BM	71A	71A	71A	-	02/62	
30853	Sir Richard Grenville	"	"	BM	71A	71A	71A	-	02/62	
30854	Howard of Effingham	"	"	BM	71A	71A	71A	-	09/61	
30855	Robert Blake	"	"	BM	71A	71A	71A	-	09/61	
30856	Lord St. Vincent	"	"	9E	71A	71A	71A	-	09/62	
30857	Lord Howe	"	"	9E	71A	71A	71A	-	09/62	
30858	Lord Duncan	"	"	9E	70A	70A	71A	-	08/61	
30859	Lord Hood	"	"	9E	70A	70A	71A	-	12/61	
30860	Lord Hawke	"	"	9E	70A	70A	71B	-	08/62	
30861	Lord Anson	"	"	9E	71B	71B	71A	-	10/62	
30862	Lord Collingwood	"	"	BM	71B	71B	71A	-	10/62	
30863	Lord Rodney	"	"	BM	71B	71B	71A	-	02/62	
30864	Sir Martin Frobisher	"	"	BM	71B	71B	71B	-	01/62	
30865	Sir John Hawkins	"	"	BM	71B	71B	71B	-	05/61	
30900	Eton	V	4-4-0	STL	74E	74E	75A	-	02/62	Never BR Green
30901	Winchester	"	"	STL	74E	74E	75A	-	12/62	
30902	Wellington	"	"	STL	74E	74E	70A	-	12/62	
30903	Charterhouse	"	"	STL	74E	74E	70A	-	12/62	
30904	Lancing	"	"	STL	74E	74E	70D	-	07/61	
30905	Tonbridge	"	"	STL	74E	74E	70D	-	12/62	
30906	Sherborne	"	"	STL	74E	74E	70A	-	12/62	
30907	Dulwich	"	"	STL	74E	74E	70A	-	09/61	
30908	Westminster	"	"	STL	74E	74E	73A	-	09/61	
30909	St. Paul's	"	"	STL	74E	74E	73A	-	02/62	
30910	Merchant Taylors	"	"	STL	74E	74E	73G	-	11/61	
30911	Dover	"	"	RAM	74B	74B	73G	-	12/62	
30912	Downside	"	"	RAM	74B	74B	73G	-	11/62	
30913	Christ's Hospital	"	"	RAM	74B	74B	73G	-	01/62	
30914	Eastbourne	"	"	RAM	74B	74B	73G	-	07/61	Never BR Green
30915	Brighton	"	"	RAM	74B	73A	73A	-	12/62	
30916	Whitgift	"	"	RAM	74B	74B	73G	-	12/62	

Number & Name	Class	W. A.	1948	1952	1955	1959	1963	w/dwn	Notes
30917 Ardingly	V	4-4-0	RAM	74B	74B	73G	-	11/62	
30918 Hurstpierpoint	"	"	RAM	74C	74B	73G	-	10/61	
30919 Harrow	"	"	RAM	74C	74C	73G	-	02/61	Never BR Green
30920 Rugby	"	"	RAM	74C	74C	73G	-	11/61	
30921 Shrewsbury	"	"	BA	74C	74C	73G	-	12/62	
30922 Marlborough	"	"	BA	75A	74B	73G	-	11/61	
30923 Bradfield	"	"	BA	74C	74C	73B	-	12/62	
30924 Haileybury	"	"	DOV	73B	73B	73B	-	01/62	
30925 Cheltenham	"	"	DOV	73B	73B	73B	-	12/62	
30926 Repton	"	"	DOV	73B	73B	73B	-	12/62	
30927 Clifton	"	"	DOV	73B	73B	73B	-	01/62	
30928 Stowe	"	"	BA	73B	73B	73B	-	11/62	
30929 Malvern	"	"	BA	73B	73B	73B	-	12/62	
30930 Radley	"	"	BA	73B	73B	73B	-	12/62	
30931 King's Wimbledon	"	"	BA	73B	73B	73B	-	09/61	
30932 Blundells	"	"	BA	73B	73B	73B	-	02/61	Never BR Green
30933 King's Canterbury	"	"	BA	73B	73B	73B	-	11/61	
30934 St. Lawrence	"	"	BA	73B	73B	73B	-	12/62	
30935 Sevenoaks	"	"	BA	73B	73B	73B	-	12/62	
30936 Cranleigh	"	"	BA	73B	73B	73B	-	12/62	
30937 Epsom	"	"	BA	73B	73B	73A	-	12/62	
30938 St. Olave's	"	"	BA	73B	73B	73A	-	07/61	
30939 Leatherhead	"	"	BA	73B	73B	73A	-	06/61	

Number	Class	W.Arrgt	1948	1952	1955	1959	1963	1966	w/dwn	Notes
30948	EKR	0-6-0T	EKR	-	-	-	-	-	02/49	Former E.K.R. No. 4
30949	KES	0-8-0T	9E	-	-	-	-	-	03/50	named 'Hecate'
30950	Z	0-8-0T	HIT	71A	74D	72A	-	-	11/62	
30951	Z	0-8-0T	HIT	73D	75E	73F	-	-	11/62	
30952	Z	0-8-0T	ELH	71A	74A	73F	-	-	11/62	
30953	Z	0-8-0T	HIT	74A	71H	82G	-	-	12/62	
30954	Z	0-8-0T	EXJ	72A	72A	72B	-	-	12/62	
30955	Z	0-8-0T	HIT	71A	74A	72A	-	-	12/62	
30956	Z	0-8-0T	HIT	71A	75A	72A	-	-	12/62	
30957	Z	0-8-0T	SAL	72B	72B	72B	-	-	11/62	
31002	F1	4-4-0	GIL	-	-	-	-	-	06/48	
31003	O1	0-6-0	GIL	-	-	-	-	-	01/49	
31004	C	0-6-0	RAM	74B	74B	73G	-	-	11/61	
31005	H	0-4-4T	BAT	73A	73A	73F	75F	-	09/63	
31007	O1	0-6-0	GIL	-	-	-	-	-	05/49	
31010	R1	0-6-0T	AFD	74A	74A	73H	-	-	08/59	
31013	B1	4-4-0	GIL	-	-	-	-	-	09/48	
31014	O1	0-6-0	GIL	-	-	-	-	-	06/48	
31016	H	0-4-4T	RAM	-	-	-	-	-	07/51	
31018	C	0-6-0	HIT	73C	73C	73C	-	-	01/59	
31019	E1	4-4-0	BAT	73A	73A	73A	-	-	04/61	
31027	P	0-6-0T	DOV	71A	74C	73H	-	-	03/61	
31028	F1	4-4-0	HIT	-	-	-	-	-	05/48	
31031	F1	4-4-0	HIT	-	-	-	-	-	05/48	
31033	C	0-6-0	BA	73C	73C	73C	-	-	03/60	
31036	E	4-4-0	BA	-	-	-	-	-	03/51	
31037	C	0-6-0	STL	74E	74A	73D	-	-	02/61	
31038	C	0-6-0	STL	74D	-	-	-	-	03/54	
31039	O1	0-6-0	GIL	-	-	-	-	-	08/49	
31041	O1	0-6-0	STL	-	-	-	-	-	05/51	
31042	F1	4-4-0	RDG	-	-	-	-	-	02/48	
31044	O1	0-6-0	HIT	-	-	-	-	-	06/51	
31046	O1	0-6-0	FAV	-	-	-	-	-	10/48	
31047	R1	0-6-0T	FOL	74C	74C	73H	-	-	03/60	

Number	Class	W.Arrgt.	1948	1952	1955	1959	1963	1966	w/dwn	Notes
31048	O1	0-6-0	TON	74A	74A	73A	-	-	10/60	
31051	O1	0-6-0	GIL	-	-	-	-	-	08/48	
31054	C	0-6-0	HIT	73C	73C	73C	-	-	08/60	
31057	D	4-4-0	TON	-	-	-	-	-	04/51	
31059	C	0-6-0	HIT	73C	73C	-	-	-	02/58	
31061	C	0-6-0	HIT	73C	73C	73C	-	-	07/61	
31063	C	0-6-0	TON	73C	73C	-	-	-	04/56	
31064	O1	0-6-0	GIL	74A	74A	-	-	-	05/58	
31065	O1	0-6-0	DOV	74A	74C	73H	-	-	06/61	
31066	O1	0-6-0	GIL	-	-	-	-	-	06/51	
31067	E1	4-4-0	BAT	73A	73A	73A	-	-	11/61	
31068	C	0-6-0	HIT	73B	73B	73B	-	-	10/61	
31069	R1	0-6-0T	AFD	74C	74C	-	-	-	06/58	
31071	C	0-6-0	HIT	73B	73B	73B	-	-	09/59	
31075	D	4-4-0	STL	70E	75B	-	-	-	12/56	
31078	F1	4-4-0	RDG	-	-	-	-	-	03/49	
31080	O1	0-6-0	RAM	-	-	-	-	-	08/49	
31086	C	0-6-0	TON	73B	73B	73B	-	-	10/60	
31090	C	0-6-0	BA	73B	-	-	-	-	08/53	
31092	D	4-4-0	GIL	-	-	-	-	-	06/51	
31093	O1	0-6-0	BA	-	-	-	-	-	05/51	
31102	C	0-6-0	BA	73B	73B	73B	-	-	05/60	
31105	F1	4-4-0	GIL	-	-	-	-	-	02/49	
31106	O1	0-6-0	FAV	-	-	-	-	-	01/49	
31107	R1	0-6-0T	FOL	74C	74C	73H	-	-	08/59	
31108	O1	0-6-0	DOV	-	-	-	-	-	07/51	
31109	O1	0-6-0	HIT	-	-	-	-	-	01/49	
31112	C	0-6-0	GIL	73D	73D	73D	-	-	04/62	
31113	C	0-6-0	HIT	74C	74C	73H	-	-	07/61	
31123	O1	0-6-0	AFD	-	-	-	-	-	01/50	
31127	R1	0-6-0T	FOL	-	-	-	-	-	01/49	
31128	R1	0-6-0T	FOL	74C	74C	73H	-	-	08/59	
31145	D1	4-4-0	BAT	74C	74C	73A	-	-	10/61	
31147	R1	0-6-0T	AFD	74A	74A	-	-	-	09/58	
31150	C	0-6-0	TON	74C	74C	73H	-	-	10/61	
31151	F1	4-4-0	RAM	-	-	-	-	-	03/49	
31154	R1	0-6-0T	FOL	74C	74C	-	-	-	09/55	
31157	E	4-4-0	HOR	-	-	-	-	-	03/51	
31158	H	0-4-4T	AFD	73A	73D	-	-	-	04/55	
31159	E	4-4-0	BA	-	-	-	-	-	12/51	
31160	E1	4-4-0	BAT	-	-	-	-	-	02/51	
31161	H	0-4-4T	DOV	74A	73D	73D	-	-	11/61	
31162	H	0-4-4T	BA	73E	74E	75E	-	-	07/61	
31163	E1	4-4-0	BAT	-	-	-	-	-	05/49	
31164	H	0-4-4T	RAM	74D	74D	73J	-	-	10/59	
31165	E1	4-4-0	BAT	73B	73B	73B	-	-	05/59	
31166	E	4-4-0	BA	73E	74D	-	-	-	05/55	
31174	R1	0-4-4T	STL	74E	74E	73H	-	-	08/59	
31175	E	4-4-0	BA	-	-	-	-	-	10/51	
31176	E	4-4-0	BA	-	-	-	-	-	10/51	
31177	H	0-4-4T	BAT	74D	74D	73J	-	-	10/61	
31178	P	0-6-0T	BTN	74C	74C	-	-	-	06/58	
31179	E1	4-4-0	BAT	-	-	-	-	-	10/50	
31182	H	0-4-4T	RAM	-	-	-	-	-	07/51	
31184	H	0-4-4T	BAT	74D	74D	-	-	-	03/58	
31191	C	0-6-0	HIT	74C	74C	73H	-	-	09/59	
31193	H	0-4-4T	TON	74D	74D	73J	-	-	03/61	
31215	F1	4-4-0	GIL	-	-	-	-	-	05/48	
31217	B1	4-4-0	RDG	-	-	-	-	-	06/50	

Number	Class	W.Arrgt.	1948	1952	1955	1959	1963	1966	w/dwn	Notes
31218	C	0-6-0	AFD	74A	74A	73F	-	-	04/62	
31219	C	0-6-0	TON	74D	74A	73F	-	-	10/59	
31221	C	0-6-0	TON	73D	74A	73F	-	-	08/59	
31223	C	0-6-0	BA	73D	74A	73F	-	-	05/60	
31225	C	0-6-0	TON	73D	73B	-	-	-	06/55	
31227	C	0-6-0	TON	73D	73D	73D	-	-	10/59	
31229	C	0-6-0	FAV	73D	73D	73D	-	-	10/61	
31231	F1	4-4-0	FAV	-	-	-	-	-	03/49	
31234	C	0-6-0	GIL	73D	-	-	-	-	08/53	
31238	O1	0-6-0	GIL	-	-	-	-	-	07/49	
31239	H	0-4-4T	AFD	74D	74D	73J	-	-	01/60	
31242	C	0-6-0	FAV	73D	73D	73E	-	-	09/61	
31243	C	0-6-0	HIT	74C	74C	73H	-	-	10/59	
31244	C	0-6-0	HIT	74D	74D	73J	-	-	10/61	
31245	C	0-6-0	HIT	74B	74B	73G	-	-	08/59	
31246	D1	4-4-0	DOV	74C	74C	73F	-	-	03/61	
31247	D1	4-4-0	BAT	74C	74C	73B	-	-	07/61	
31248	O1	0-6-0	HIT	-	-	-	-	-	06/51	
31252	C	0-6-0	DOV	74B	74B	73G	-	-	07/59	
31253	C	0-6-0	HIT	73E	70C	73C	-	-	10/59	
31255	C	0-6-0	DOV	73E	73E	73E	-	-	09/61	
31256	C	0-6-0	GIL	73E	73E	73E	-	-	07/61	
31257	C	0-6-0	HIT	-	-	-	-	-	08/49	
31258	OI	0-6-0	HIT	74C	74C	73H	-	-	02/61	
31259	H	0-4-4T	BAT	74D	74D	73J	-	-	11/59	
31260	C	0-6-0	FAV	73E	-	-	-	-	05/53	
31261	H	0-4-4T	AFD	73A	73A	73A	-	-	10/61	
31263	H	0-4-4T	BAT	73A	73A	73F	75F	-	01/64	
31265	H	0-4-4T	RAM	73A	73A	73A	-	-	08/60	
31266	H	0-4-4T	BAT	73A	73A	73J	-	-	10/60	
31267	C	0-6-0	GIL	73E	73B	73B	-	-	06/62	
31268	C	0-6-0	AFD	73E	73E	73E	-	-	04/62	
31269	H	0-4-4T	AFD	73A	74E	75E	-	-	12/59	
31270	C	0-6-0	HIT	74D	74D	73J	-	-	06/59	
31271	C	0-6-0	AFD	74B	74B	73G	-	-	07/63	
31272	C	0-6-0	TON	74D	74D	73J	-	-	08/59	
31273	E	4-4-0	HOR	-	-	-	-	-	12/51	
31274	H	0-4-4T	AFD	74C	74E	-	-	-	11/57	
31275	E	4-4-0	BA	-	-	-	-	-	03/51	
31276	H	0-4-4T	DOV	74B	74A	73F	-	-	02/61	
31277	C	0-6-0	BA	74D	74D	-	-	-	09/55	
31278	H	0-4-4T	GIL	74A	74C	75F	-	-	10/62	
31279	H	0-4-4T	FAV	74E	74E	73J	-	-	09/59	
31280	C	0-6-0	BA	73B	73B	73J	-	-	07/63	
31287	C	0-6-0	BA	73B	73B	73C	-	-	10/60	
31291	C	0-6-0	DOV	73B	-	-	-	-	05/53	
31293	C	0-6-0	BAT	73B	73B	73B	-	-	04/62	
31294	C	0-6-0	BA	73B	73B	-	-	-	10/55	
31295	H	0-4-4T	BAT	73D	74E	73J	-	-	05/59	
31297	C	0-6-0	BA	73B	73B	73D	-	-	09/59	
31298	C	0-6-0	HIT	74B	74B	73E	-	-	11/60	
31302	1302	0-4-0CT	BAT	-	-	-	-	-	07/49	
31305	H	0-4-4T	AFD	73D	73E	73B	-	-	11/62	
31306	H	0-4-4T	AFD	73D	73B	73B	-	-	12/61	
31307	H	0-4-4T	BAT	73D	73D	73F	-	-	08/61	
31308	H	0-4-4T	GIL	73D	73D	73D	-	-	12/62	
31309	H	0-4-4T	FAV	75B	75B	-	-	-	06/55	
31310	H	0-4-4T	FAV	75B	75A	75F	-	-	05/60	
31311	H	0-4-4T	BAT	73A	-	-	-	-	12/54	

Number	Class	W.Arrgt.	1948	1952	1955	1959	1963	1966	w/dwn	Notes
31315	E	4-4-0	BA	73E	-	-	-	-	03/54	
31316	O1	0-6-0	RAM	-	-	-	-	-	06/49	
31317	C	0-6-0	GIL	74C	74C	73A	-	-	02/62	
31319	H	0-4-4T	BAT	73A	75A	73F	-	-	01/60	
31320	H	0-4-4T	TON	73A	75A	-	-	-	12/55	
31321	H	0-4-4T	BAT	73A	73A	-	-	-	11/57	
31322	H	0-4-4T	AFD	75F	75F	73D	-	-	04/61	
31323	P	0-6-0T	FOL	74C	74C	73H	-	-	07/60	
31324	H	0-4-4T	BA	74B	74B	73G	-	-	07/62	
31325	P	0-6-0T	DOV	75A	75A	75A	-	-	03/60	
31326	H	0-4-4T	BA	74B	74B	73G	-	-	10/61	
31327	H	0-4-4T	TON	74A	74A	75F	-	-	11/59	
31328	H	0-4-4T	BA	74C	74C	73H	-	-	02/61	
31329	H	0-4-4T	BAT	73E	74C	75F	-	-	11/59	
31335	R1	0-6-0T	STL	74E	74E	-	-	-	07/55	
31337	R1	0-6-0T	FOL	74C	74C	73H	-	-	02/60	
31339	R1	0-6-0T	AFD	74A	74A	-	-	-	06/58	
31340	R1	0-6-0T	FOL	74C	74C	73H	-	-	02/59	
31369	O1	0-6-0	FAV	-	-	-	-	-	09/51	
31370	O1	0-6-0	TON	74A	74A	73A	-	-	02/60	
31371	O1	0-6-0	EKR	-	-	-	-	-	01/49	was East Kent Railway No. 1371
31372	O1	0-6-0	EKR	-	-	-	-	-	02/49	was East Kent Railway No. 6
31373	O1	0-6-0	DOV	-	-	-	-	-	07/51	
31374	O1	0-6-0	HIT	-	-	-	-	-	09/49	
31377	O1	0-6-0	HIT	-	-	-	-	-	01/50	
31378	O1	0-6-0	GIL	-	-	-	-	-	11/48	
31379	O1	0-6-0	FAV	-	-	-	-	-	05/51	
31380	O1	0-6-0	TON	-	-	-	-	-	11/49	
31381	O1	0-6-0	DOV	-	-	-	-	-	05/51	
31383	O1	0-6-0	EKR	-	-	-	-	-	04/51	was East Kent Railway No. 2
31384	O1	0-6-0	GIL	-	-	-	-	-	12/49	
31385	O1	0-6-0	HIT	-	-	-	-	-	09/49	
31386	O1	0-6-0	HIT	-	-	-	-	-	10/48	
31388	O1	0-6-0	BA	-	-	-	-	-	07/48	
31389	O1	0-6-0	BA	-	-	-	-	-	02/49	
31390	O1	0-6-0	AFD	-	-	-	-	-	05/51	
31391	O1	0-6-0	GIL	-	-	-	-	-	06/51	
31395	O1	0-6-0	BA	-	-	-	-	-	06/51	
31396	O1	0-6-0	TON	-	-	-	-	-	08/48	
31397	O1	0-6-0	BA	-	-	-	-	-	06/48	
31398	O1	0-6-0	BA	-	-	-	-	-	05/49	
31400	N	2-6-0	AFD	74A	74A	73F	75A	-	06/64	
31401	N	2-6-0	AFD	74A	74A	73F	75A	-	07/65	
31402	N	2-6-0	AFD	74A	74A	73F	75A	-	08/63	
31403	N	2-6-0	AFD	74A	74A	73F	75A	-	06/63	
31404	N	2-6-0	AFD	74A	74A	73F	70E	-	12/63	
31405	N	2-6-0	BAT	74A	74A	73F	71G	70C	06/66	
31406	N	2-6-0	RED	74A	74A	73F	72A	-	09/64	
31407	N	2-6-0	EXJ	74A	74A	73F	71G	-	07/63	
31408	N	2-6-0	EXJ	74A	74B	73A	70E	70C	06/66	
31409	N	2-6-0	EXJ	73A	73A	73A	-	-	10/62	
31410	N	2-6-0	BAT	73A	73A	73A	75D	-	11/64	
31411	N	2-6-0	BAT	73A	73A	73A	75D	70C	04/66	
31412	N	2-6-0	BAT	73A	73A	73A	57D	-	08/64	
31413	N	2-6-0	BAT	73A	73A	73A	71A	-	06/64	
31414	N	2-6-0	BAT	73A	73A	73A	-	-	11/62	
31425	O1	0-6-0	BA	74C	74C	73H	-	-	08/59	
31426	O1	0-6-0	AFD	-	-	-	-	-	08/48	
31428	O1	0-6-0	BA	-	-	-	-	-	03/49	

Number	Class	W.Arrgt.	1948	1952	1955	1959	1963	1966	w/dwn	Notes
31429	O1	0-6-0	BA	-	-	-	-	-	09/49	
31430	O1	0-6-0	GIL	74C	74C	73H	-	-	05/59	
31432	O1	0-6-0	STL	-	-	-	-	-	06/51	
31434	O1	0-6-0	AFD	74C	74C	73H	-	-	08/59	
31437	O1	0-6-0	TON	-	-	-	-	-	10/48	
31438	O1	0-6-0	FAV	-	-	-	-	-	11/48	
31439	O1	0-6-0	GIL	-	-	-	-	-	05/49	
31440	B1	4-4-0	FAV	-	-	-	-	-	11/48	
31443	B1	4-4-0	DOV	-	-	-	-	-	03/51	
31445	B1	4-4-0	BAT	-	-	-	-	-	02/48	
31446	B1	4-4-0	RDG	-	-	-	-	-	07/49	
31448	B1	4-4-0	FAV	-	-	-	-	-	08/49	
31449	B1	4-4-0	GIL	-	-	-	-	-	03/49	
31450	B1	4-4-0	DOV	-	-	-	-	-	04/48	
31451	B1	4-4-0	RAM	-	-	-	-	-	12/49	
31452	B1	4-4-0	RAM	-	-	-	-	-	04/50	
31453	B1	4-4-0	RAM	-	-	-	-	-	10/48	
31454	B1	4-4-0	BAT	-	-	-	-	-	11/48	
31455	B1	4-4-0	HIT	-	-	-	-	-	06/49	
31457	B1	4-4-0	HIT	-	-	-	-	-	02/49	
31459	B1	4-4-0	RDG	-	-	-	-	-	02/48	
31460	C	0-6-0	BA	-	-	-	-	-	02/49	
31461	C	0-6-0	TON	73E	73A	-	-	-	08/58	
31470	D1	4-4-0	DOV	74C	73E	73J	-	-	06/59	
31477	D	4-4-0	AFD	-	-	-	-	-	02/51	
31480	C	0-6-0	HIT	73C	73C	73B	-	-	07/61	
31481	C	0-6-0	FAV	73E	73E	73E	-	-	11/61	
31486	C	0-6-0	HIT	73C	-	-	-	-	05/53	
31487	D1	4-4-0	FAV	73E	73E	73J	-	-	02/61	
31488	D	4-4-0	TON	70E	70E	-	-	-	02/56	
31489	D1	4-4-0	FAV	73E	73E	73J	-	-	11/61	
31490	D	4-4-0	TON	-	-	-	-	-	09/51	
31491	E	4-4-0	BA	75B	-	-	-	-	02/53	
31492	D1	4-4-0	BAT	73E	73E	73J	-	-	01/60	
31493	D	4-4-0	FAV	74E	-	-	-	-	02/54	
31494	D1	4-4-0	BAT	73E	73E	73E	-	-	08/60	
31495	C	0-6-0	FAV	73D	73D	73D	-	-	03/61	
31496	D	4-4-0	FAV	74E	70C	-	-	-	09/55	
31497	E1	4-4-0	BAT	73B	73B	73B	-	-	10/60	
31498	C	0-6-0	BAT	73D	73C	73C	-	-	07/61	
31500	H	0-4-4T	BA	73E	74A	73G	-	-	06/61	
31501	D	4-4-0	FAV	73D	-	-	-	-	05/53	
31502	D1	4-4-0	FAV	-	-	-	-	-	03/51	
31503	H	0-4-4T	TON	73E	73E	73E	-	-	08/59	
31504	E1	4-4-0	BAT	73A	73A	-	-	-	02/58	
31505	D1	4-4-0	FAV	73E	73D	73E	-	-	09/61	
31506	E1	4-4-0	BAT	73A	73A	-	-	-	09/58	
31507	E1	4-4-0	BAT	73B	73B	73B	-	-	07/61	
31508	C	0-6-0	BAT	73D	73D	-	-	-	09/57	
31509	D1	4-4-0	FAV	73D	73D	73E	-	-	05/60	
31510	C	0-6-0	GIL	73D	73D	73D	-	-	06/62	
31511	E1	4-4-0	BAT	-	-	-	-	-	12/50	
31512	H	0-4-4T	DOV	74A	74A	73D	-	-	06/61	
31513	C	0-6-0	TON	74A	74A	-	-	-	03/55	
31514	E	4-4-0	BAT	-	-	-	-	-	12/51	
31515	E	4-4-0	BAT	-	-	-	-	-	07/51	
31516	E	4-4-0	BAT	-	-	-	-	-	10/51	
31517	H	0-4-4T	DOV	75F	75F	73J	-	-	05/61	
31518	H	0-4-4T	TON	74E	73D	73D	75F	-	01/64	

Number	Class	W.Arrgt.	1948	1952	1955	1959	1963	1966	w/dwn	Notes
31519	H	0-4-4T	TON	74E	74E	73F	-	-	02/61	
31520	H	0-4-4T	DOV	75F	75F	73F	-	-	08/60	
31521	H	0-4-4T	RAM	74C	74A	75F	-	-	05/62	
31522	H	0-4-4T	RAM	74A	74A	73F	-	-	01/63	
31523	H	0-4-4T	RAM	74D	74D	73J	-	-	01/59	
31530	H	0-4-4T	DOV	74C	74D	75E	-	-	03/62	
31531	H	0-4-4T	DOV	74C	74C	-	-	-	04/55	
31532	H	0-4-4T	DOV	-	-	-	-	-	03/51	
31533	H	0-4-4T	BA	73B	73B	73B	-	-	09/62	
31540	H	0-4-4T	TON	73B	73B	73B	-	-	02/60	
31541	H	0-4-4T	BA	-	-	-	-	-	04/51	
31542	H	0-4-4T	BA	73B	73B	73H	-	-	11/62	
31543	H	0-4-4T	TON	73B	74D	73J	75F	-	07/63	
31544	H	0-4-4T	9E	73B	74D	75F	75F	-	09/63	
31545	D1	4-4-0	DOV	73D	73D	73A	-	-	03/61	
31546	H	0-4-4T	BA	-	-	-	-	-	02/51	
31547	E	4-4-0	BA	-	-	-	-	-	02/51	
31548	H	0-4-4T	DOV	74D	74D	73D	-	-	08/59	
31549	D	4-4-0	AFD	74A	74A	-	-	-	10/56	
31550	H	0-4-4T	BA	70A	73A	73A	-	-	02/61	
31551	H	0-4-4T	9E	70A	73A	73A	75F	-	01/64	
31552	H	0-4-4T	9E	70A	73A	73A	-	-	11/61	
31553	H	0-4-4T	9E	70A	73B	73B	-	-	06/61	
31554	H	0-4-4T	BAT	74D	74D	75F	-	-	05/59	
31555	P	0-6-0T	DOV	74C	73A	-	-	-	02/55	
31556	P	0-6-0T	DOV	75A	75A	75A	-	-	06/61	
31557	P	0-6-0T	BTN	73A	73A	-	-	-	09/57	
31558	P	0-6-0T	FOL	73A	75A	73A	-	-	02/60	
31572	C	0-6-0	HIT	74A	-	-	-	-	03/54	
31573	C	0-6-0	GIL	73A	73A	73C	-	-	11/61	
31574	D	4-4-0	AFD	74A	74A	-	-	-	10/56	
31575	C	0-6-0	BAT	73A	73A	73A	-	-	07/61	
31576	C	0-6-0	BAT	73A	73A	73D	-	-	11/59	
31577	D	4-4-0	AFD	74A	74A	-	-	-	12/56	
31578	C	0-6-0	BAT	73A	73A	73A	-	-	06/61	
31579	C	0-6-0	GIL	73A	73A	73D	-	-	10/61	
31580	C	0-6-0	TON	73A	-	-	-	-	08/53	
31581	C	0-6-0	HIT	73A	73A	73A	-	-	03/60	
31582	C	0-6-0	BAT	73A	73A	-	-	-	06/58	
31583	C	0-6-0	GIL	73A	73A	73A	-	-	07/61	
31584	C	0-6-0	BA	73A	73A	73A	-	-	02/62	
31585	C	0-6-0	GIL	74D	74D	73J	-	-	02/59	
31586	D	4-4-0	TON	75B	70C	-	-	-	09/55	
31587	E	4-4-0	RED	-	-	-	-	-	07/51	
31588	C	0-6-0	GIL	74D	74D	73J	-	-	06/62	
31589	C	0-6-0	AFD	74A	74A	73F	-	-	11/61	
31590	C	0-6-0	TON	74D	74D	73J	-	-	02/61	
31591	D	4-4-0	TON	75B	75B	-	-	-	06/55	
31592	C	0-6-0	RAM	74B	74B	73G	-	-	07/63	
31593	C	0-6-0	TON	73D	70C	-	-	-	02/58	
31595	J	0-6-4T	AFD	-	-	-	-	-	05/51	
31596	J	0-6-4T	AFD	-	-	-	-	-	10/51	
31597	J	0-6-4T	AFD	-	-	-	-	-	11/50	
31598	J	0-6-4T	AFD	-	-	-	-	-	12/50	
31599	J	0-6-4T	AFD	-	-	-	-	-	10/49	
31602	T	0-6-0T	BAT	-	-	-	-	-	07/51	
31604	T	0-6-0T	BAT	-	-	-	-	-	12/50	
31610	U	2-6-0	RDG	70E	72C	72C	-	-	12/62	
31611	U	2-6-0	RDG	70E	75B	71A	70D	-	10/63	
								-		

Class E4 0-6-2T No. 32487, with plenty of coal in the bunker, looks very clean and smart as it poses for the cameraman. Look where the shovel is kept - how do you get it out of there easily?

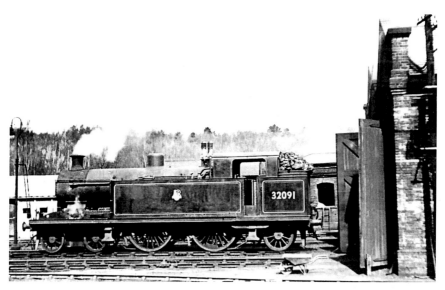

Class I3 No. 32091 was the final development of L.B.S.C. 4-4-2Ts, and was built new with a superheater and increased cylinder diameter. It was withdrawn during June 1952 from Brighton shed after almost forty years service.

Number	Class	W.Arrgt.	1948	1952	1955	1959	1963	1966	w/dwn	Notes
31612	U	2-6-0	SAL	70E	75B	70C	70A	-	05/63	▾
31613	U	2-6-0	9E	70E	71A	71A	70A	-	01/64	
31614	U	2-6-0	GFD	70E	75B	71B	72C	-	11/63	
31615	U	2-6-0	RDG	70E	75B	71B	70C	-	10/63	
31616	U	2-6-0	9E	70E	70C	70C	75C	-	06/64	
31617	U	2-6-0	9E	70E	70A	70A	70A	-	01/64	
31618	U	2-6-0	SAL	70E	71A	71A	70D	-	01/64	
31619	U	2-6-0	9E	73C	71A	71A	75C	-	12/65	
31620	U	2-6-0	RDG	73C	71A	71A	75C	-	04/65	
31621	U	2-6-0	GFD	73C	71A	70A	70A	-	06/64	
31622	U	2-6-0	BM	71B	70C	70C	70C	-	01/64	
31623	U	2-6-0	GFD	71B	72C	72C	70C	-	12/63	
31624	U	2-6-0	BM	70C	70C	70A	70A	-	06/64	
31625	U	2-6-0	EXJ	70C	70C	70C	70C	-	01/64	
31626	U	2-6-0	SAL	70C	71A	72A	75C	-	01/64	
31627	U	2-6-0	BAS	70C	70C	70C	70C	-	10/65	
31628	U	2-6-0	RDG	70C	70C	70C	70C	-	06/64	
31629	U	2-6-0	BAS	70C	70A	71A	75C	-	01/64	
31630	U	2-6-0	SAL	70C	70C	70C	-	-	11/62	
31631	U	2-6-0	FAV	71C	70C	70C	70C	-	09/63	
31632	U	2-6-0	BAS	71C	71C	71B	72C	-	09/64	
31633	U	2-6-0	BAS	70D	70D	71A	70C	-	12/63	
31634	U	2-6-0	BAS	70D	70D	70A	70A	-	12/63	
31635	U	2-6-0	EXJ	72B	72B	70C	70C	-	12/63	
31636	U	2-6-0	SAL	72B	72B	70C	70A	-	06/63	
31637	U	2-6-0	9E	73E	70F	70F	72C	-	09/63	
31638	U	2-6-0	EXJ	71A	70F	70F	70C	-	01/64	
31639	U	2-6-0	FAV	72C	72B	71A	75C	70C	06/66	
31658	R	0-4-4T	GIL	73D	-	-	-	-	12/52	
31659	R	0-4-4T	GIL	-	-	-	-	-	09/51	
31660	R	0-4-4T	GIL	73D	-	-	-	-	12/53	
31661	R	0-4-4T	BAT	73E	74C	-	-	-	09/55	
31662	R	0-4-4T	GIL	73D	-	-	-	-	10/53	
31663	R	0-4-4T	GIL	73D	-	-	-	-	07/53	
31665	R	0-4-4T	GIL	74D	-	-	-	-	10/52	
31666	R	0-4-4T	GIL	74D	74D	-	-	-	12/55	
31667	R	0-4-4T	FAV	-	-	-	-	-	04/51	
31670	R	0-4-4T	TON	-	-	-	-	-	04/51	
31671	R	0-4-4T	TON	74D	-	-	-	-	11/54	
31672	R	0-4-4T	TON	-	-	-	-	-	12/49	
31673	R	0-4-4T	DOV	74C	-	-	-	-	10/52	
31674	R	0-4-4T	FAV	-	-	-	-	-	06/52	
31675	R	0-4-4T	TON	74D	-	-	-	-	12/52	
31681	C	0-6-0	BAT	73D	73D	73D	-	-	02/59	
31682	C	0-6-0	GIL	73D	73D	73D	-	-	10/61	
31683	C	0-6-0	BAT	73D	73D	73D	-	-	06/59	
31684	C	0-6-0	GIL	73D	73D	73D	-	-	10/61	
31685	S	0-6-0ST	BA	-	-	-	-	-	10/51	
31686	C	0-6-0	TON	73C	73C	73C	-	-	04/62	
31687	C	0-6-0	BA	73C	73C	-	-	-	04/55	
31688	C	0-6-0	GIL	73C	73C	73C	-	-	02/60	
31689	C	0-6-0	HIT	73C	73C	73C	-	-	03/62	
31690	C	0-6-0	BAT	73C	73C	73C	-	-	06/62	
31691	C	0-6-0	FAV	73C	73C	73C	-	-	10/61	
31692	C	0-6-0	FAV	73C	73C	73C	-	-	04/60	
31693	C	0-6-0	BA	73C	73C	73C	-	-	06/61	
31694	C	0-6-0	BAT	73C	73C	73C	-	-	03/61	
31695	C	0-6-0	HIT	73C	73C	73C	-	-	06/61	
31696	R1	0-4-4T	FEL	-	-	-	-	-	03/51	

An unidentified Class 'N' 2-6-0 in Southern Railway livery hauls a very long freight train - so long that it disappears off the photograph! Note the seemingly indiscriminate mix of vans and open wagons ; in reality they will have been prepared in exact running order for 'cutting' into subsequent trains to their final destinations

Number	Class	W.Arrgt.	1948	1952	1955	1959	1963	1966	w/dwn	Notes
31697	R1	0-4-4T	GIL	73D	-	-	-	-	03/53	
31698	R1	0-4-4T	FEL	73E	74D	-	-	-	10/55	
31699	R1	0-4-4T	FAV	-	-	-	-	-	01/50	
31700	R1	0-4-4T	TON	74D	-	-	-	-	10/52	
31703	R1	0-4-4T	TON	74D	-	-	-	-	03/54	
31704	R1	0-4-4T	TON	74D	74D	-	-	-	04/56	
31705	R1	0-4-4T	DOV	-	-	-	-	-	06/51	
31706	R1	0-4-4T	BAT	74D	-	-	-	-	12/52	
31707	R1	0-4-4T	TON	-	-	-	-	-	02/49	
31708	R1	0-4-4T	DOV	73E	-	-	-	-	10/52	
31709	R1	0-4-4T	FAV	-	-	-	-	-	10/49	
31710	R1	0-4-4T	BAT	-	-	-	-	-	06/51	
31711	C	0-6-0	AFD	74A	73D	-	-	-	01/57	
31712	C	0-6-0	BAT	73D	73D	-	-	-	02/57	
31713	C	0-6-0	GIL	73D	73D	-	-	-	04/55	
31714	C	0-6-0	BAT	73E	73E	73E	-	-	07/61	
31715	C	0-6-0	FAV	73E	73E	73E	-	-	11/61	
31716	C	0-6-0	BAT	74D	74D	73J	-	-	10/61	
31717	C	0-6-0	BAT	74D	74D	73B	-	-	02/62	
31718	C	0-6-0	BAT	73A	73A	-	-	-	09/55	
31719	C	0-6-0	BAT	73A	73A	73A	-	-	05/62	
31720	C	0-6-0	HIT	73B	73E	73D	-	-	10/61	
31721	C	0-6-0	AFD	73A	74E	73C	-	-	03/62	
31722	C	0-6-0	BAT	73B	73B	70C	-	-	04/62	
31723	C	0-6-0	BA	73B	73B	70C	-	-	01/62	
31724	C	0-6-0	BA	73B	75E	75A	-	-	04/62	
31725	C	0-6-0	BA	73B	75D	75A	-	-	08/60	
31727	D1	4-4-0	DOV	74D	74D	73F	-	-	03/61	
31728	D	4-4-0	RED	74D	-	-	-	-	05/53	
31729	D	4-4-0	RED	73D	-	-	-	-	05/54	
31730	D	4-4-0	HOR	-	-	-	-	-	03/51	
31731	D	4-4-0	TON	-	-	-	-	-	06/51	
31732	D	4-4-0	TON	-	-	-	-	-	09/51	
31733	D	4-4-0	TON	74D	-	-	-	-	12/53	
31734	D	4-4-0	TON	74D	74D	-	-	-	11/55	
31735	D	4-4-0	DOV	74A	73B	73B	-	-	04/61	
31736	D1	4-4-0	BAT	-	-	-	-	-	12/50	
31737	D	4-4-0	STL	70E	74D	-	-	-	10/56	
31738	D	4-4-0	STL	-	-	-	-	-	10/50	
31739	D1	4-4-0	FAV	74D	73B	73B	-	-	11/61	
31740	D	4-4-0	STL	-	-	-	-	-	03/51	
31741	D1	4-4-0	FAV	73B	73B	73B	-	-	09/59	
31743	D1	4-4-0	BAT	73A	73A	73A	-	-	02/60	
31744	D	4-4-0	STL	70E	-	-	-	-	05/53	
31745	D1	4-4-0	BAT	-	-	-	-	-	03/51	
31746	D	4-4-0	GIL	70E	-	-	-	-	12/54	
31748	D	4-4-0	AFD	-	-	-	-	-	03/51	
31749	D1	4-4-0	BAT	73A	73A	73A	-	-	11/61	
31750	D	4-4-0	GIL	70E	-	-	-	-	02/53	
31753	L1	4-4-0	DOV	74C	74C	73H	-	-	10/61	
31754	L1	4-4-0	DOV	74C	74C	73H	-	-	11/61	
31755	L1	4-4-0	DOV	74C	74C	73H	-	-	08/59	
31756	L1	4-4-0	DOV	74C	74A	73F	-	-	10/61	
31757	L1	4-4-0	DOV	74C	74A	73F	-	-	12/61	
31758	L1	4-4-0	BA	73A	74A	73F	-	-	10/59	
31759	L1	4-4-0	BA	73A	74A	73F	-	-	11/61	
31760	L	4-4-0	BAT	74D	74D	73J	-	-	06/61	
31761	L	4-4-0	TON	74D	74D	-	-	-	12/56	
31762	L	4-4-0	TON	74D	74D	73J	-	-	02/60	

Another Drummond masterpiece was the 'T9' Class, and none of the other 4-4-0 classes which followed on the L.S.W.R. lasted as long as they did.

They were nicknamed 'Greyhounds' on account of their free steaming and good turn of speed, and No. 30313, shown above at Exmouth Junction Shed, lasted in service until July 1961.

L.B.S.C.R. Class A1X 'Terrier' 0-6-0T No. 32636, built as No. 72 FENCHURCH in November 1872, was withdrawn from B.R. service during November 1963, after a working life of NINETY ONE years!

Number	Class	W.Arrgt.	1948	1952	1955	1959	1963	1966	w/dwn	Notes
31763	L	4-4-0	TON	74D	74D	73J	-	-	04/60	
31764	L	4-4-0	BAT	74D	74E	73G	-	-	02/61	
31765	L	4-4-0	BAT	74D	74D	73E	-	-	02/61	
31766	L	4-4-0	STL	74E	74D	73E	-	-	02/61	
31767	L	4-4-0	STL	74E	74E	73E	-	-	10/58	
31768	L	4-4-0	STL	74A	74E	73E	-	-	12/61	
31769	L	4-4-0	BAT	74E	74E	-	-	-	04/56	
31770	L	4-4-0	AFD	74A	74D	73J	-	-	11/59	
31771	L	4-4-0	AFD	74A	74D	73J	-	-	12/61	
31772	L	4-4-0	AFD	74A	74A	73J	-	-	02/59	
31773	L	4-4-0	AFD	74A	74D	73J	-	-	08/59	
31774	L	4-4-0	AFD	71A	74A	73J	-	-	12/58	
31775	L	4-4-0	AFD	71A	74A	73G	-	-	08/59	
31776	L	4-4-0	AFD	71A	74A	75A	-	-	02/61	
31777	L	4-4-0	RAM	71A	74A	75A	-	-	09/59	
31778	L	4-4-0	RAM	71A	74A	75A	-	-	08/59	
31779	L	4-4-0	RAM	74B	74B	73G	-	-	07/59	
31780	L	4-4-0	RAM	74B	74B	73G	-	-	07/61	
31781	L	4-4-0	RAM	74B	74B	73G	-	-	06/59	
31782	L1	4-4-0	BA	73B	74A	73F	-	-	02/61	
31783	L1	4-4-0	BA	73B	73B	73B	-	-	11/61	
31784	L1	4-4-0	BA	73B	73B	73B	-	-	02/60	
31785	L1	4-4-0	BA	73B	73B	73D	-	-	01/60	
31786	L1	4-4-0	BA	73B	73B	73D	-	-	02/62	
31787	L1	4-4-0	BA	73B	73B	73D	-	-	01/61	
31788	L1	4-4-0	BA	73B	73B	73H	-	-	01/60	
31789	L1	4-4-0	BA	73B	73B	73H	-	-	11/61	
31790	U	2-6-0	YEO	72C	72C	72A	70C	-	05/65	
31791	U	2-6-0	YEO	72C	72C	72A	71A	70C	06/66	
31792	U	2-6-0	YEO	72C	72C	71A	72C	-	09/64	
31793	U	2-6-0	YEO	72C	72C	71A	71A	-	05/64	
31794	U	2-6-0	YEO	72C	72C	71A	71A	-	06/63	
31795	U	2-6-0	YEO	72C	72C	71A	71A	-	06/63	
31796	U	2-6-0	BM	72C	72C	71A	70A	-	01/64	
31797	U	2-6-0	FRA	70C	70C	70C	70C	-	01/64	
31798	U	2-6-0	GFD	70C	70C	70C	72C	-	09/64	
31799	U	2-6-0	GFD	70C	70C	70C	75C	-	02/65	
31800	U	2-6-0	GFD	70C	70C	70C	70C	-	10/65	
31801	U	2-6-0	GFD	70C	71A	71A	71A	-	06/64	
31802	U	2-6-0	GFD	70C	73E	71A	72C	-	09/64	
31803	U	2-6-0	GFD	73E	73E	71A	71A	70C	03/66	
31804	U	2-6-0	GFD	73E	73E	70F	71A	-	06/64	
31805	U	2-6-0	GFD	71A	70F	70F	72C	-	08/63	
31806	U	2-6-0	GFD	73E	70A	70D	70D	-	01/64	
31807	U	2-6-0	RDG	71D	70F	70F	75C	-	01/64	
31808	U	2-6-0	FAV	71A	70F	70F	71A	-	01/64	
31809	U	2-6-0	GFD	71D	70F	70F	71A	70C	01/66	
31810	N	2-6-0	BAT	73A	73A	73A	71A	-	03/64	
31811	N	2-6-0	BAT	73A	73A	73A	70C	-	07/65	
31812	N	2-6-0	BAT	73A	73A	73A	70C	-	07/64	
31813	N	2-6-0	BAT	73A	72B	72B	70E	-	10/63	
31814	N	2-6-0	NOR	73A	72B	72B	70E	-	07/64	
31815	N	2-6-0	RED	73D	73D	73D	70C	-	05/63	
31816	N	2-6-0	RED	73D	73D	73D	71A	70C	01/66	
31817	N	2-6-0	RED	74C	74C	75B	75B	-	01/64	
31818	N	2-6-0	RED	74C	74C	73H	72A	-	09/63	
31819	N	2-6-0	DOV	74C	74C	73H	70C	-	01/64	
31820	N	2-6-0	DOV	74C	74C	73H	70C	-	09/63	
31821	N	2-6-0	DOV	74C	74C	73H	70C	-	05/64	

Rebuilt 'Merchant Navy' Class 4-6-2 No. 35022 Holland - America Line was built in October 1948, and withdrawn during May 1966, after eighteen years in service.

The Bulleid Pacifics, like the B.R. Standard 4-6-2s and L.N.E.R. designed A1s and A2s, were all scrapped long before their potential working lives were ended. What a pity they couldn't have lasted another few years!

Rebuilt 'Battle of Britain' Class 4-6-2 No. 34088 213 Squadron arriving at Waterloo. No. 34088 was withdrawn from Basingstoke (70D) during March 1967.

Number	Class	W.Arrgt.	1948	1952	1955	1959	1963	1966	w/dwn	Notes
31822	N1	2-6-0	STL	73C	73C	73C	-	-	11/62	
31823	N	2-6-0	DOV	73B	73B	73B	75D	-	09/63	
31824	N	2-6-0	BA	73B	73B	73B	75D	-	10/63	
31825	N	2-6-0	BA	73B	73B	73B	75D	-	09/63	
31826	N	2-6-0	BA	73B	73B	73B	75D	-	09/63	
31827	N	2-6-0	ELH	73B	73B	73B	75A	-	06/64	
31828	N	2-6-0	EXJ	73B	73B	73B	75A	-	09/64	
31829	N	2-6-0	ELH	73B	73B	73B	75A	-	01/64	
31830	N	2-6-0	TON	72A	72A	72A	75A	-	01/64	
31831	N	2-6-0	FRA	72A	72A	72A	75A	-	04/65	
31832	N	2-6-0	EXJ	72A	72A	72A	75A	-	01/64	
31833	N	2-6-0	EXJ	72A	72A	72A	75A	-	02/64	
31834	N	2-6-0	EXJ	72A	72A	72A	72A	-	09/64	
31835	N	2-6-0	EXJ	72A	72A	72A	72A	-	09/64	
31836	N	2-6-0	EXJ	72A	72A	72A	72A	-	12/63	
31837	N	2-6-0	EXJ	72A	72A	72A	72A	-	09/64	
31838	N	2-6-0	EXJ	72A	72A	72A	72A	-	02/64	
31839	N	2-6-0	EXJ	72A	72A	72A	72A	-	12/63	
31840	N	2-6-0	EXJ	72E	72A	72A	72A	-	09/64	
31841	N	2-6-0	EXJ	72E	72A	72A	72A	-	03/64	
31842	N	2-6-0	EXJ	72E	72E	72A	72A	-	09/65	
31843	N	2-6-0	RED	72A	72E	72A	72A	-	09/64	
31844	N	2-6-0	NOR	72A	72A	72A	72A	-	12/63	
31845	N	2-6-0	EXJ	72A	72A	72A	72A	-	09/64	
31846	N	2-6-0	SAL	72A	72A	72A	72A	-	09/64	
31847	N	2-6-0	EXJ	72A	72A	72A	72A	-	10/63	
31848	N	2-6-0	SAL	72A	72A	73F	72A	-	02/64	
31849	N	2-6-0	RED	72A	72A	72A	72A	-	07/64	
31850	N	2-6-0	RDG	73E	73E	73E	75B	-	01/64	
31851	N	2-6-0	RED	71D	72A	73B	75B	-	09/63	
31852	N	2-6-0	RED	71D	73E	73E	75B	-	09/63	
31853	N	2-6-0	EXJ	73B	73B	73B	72A	-	09/64	
31854	N	2-6-0	RDG	73E	73C	73F	75D	-	06/64	
31855	N	2-6-0	EXJ	73B	73C	73C	72A	-	09/64	
31856	N	2-6-0	EXJ	73C	73C	73C	72A	-	07/64	
31857	N	2-6-0	RDG	73C	73C	73C	70C	-	01/64	
31858	N	2-6-0	RED	73C	73C	73C	70C	-	12/65	
31859	N	2-6-0	TON	73C	73C	73C	70C	-	09/64	
31860	N	2-6-0	RDG	73C	73C	73C	72A	-	11/63	
31861	N	2-6-0	RDG	73C	73C	73C	75B	-	05/63	
31862	N	2-6-0	TON	73C	75B	75B	75B	-	04/65	
31863	N	2-6-0	RED	75B	75B	75B	75B	-	07/63	
31864	N	2-6-0	RED	75B	75B	75B	75B	-	01/64	
31865	N	2-6-0	BA	75B	75B	75B	75B	-	09/63	
31866	N	2-6-0	ELH	75B	75B	75B	75B	70C	01/66	
31867	N	2-6-0	ELH	75B	75B	75B	75B	-	07/63	
31868	N	2-6-0	RDG	75B	75B	75B	75B	-	01/64	
31869	N	2-6-0	EXJ	75B	75B	75B	75B	-	08/64	
31870	N	2-6-0	ELH	73B	73B	73B	75B	-	04/64	
31871	N	2-6-0	EXJ	73B	73B	73B	75B	-	11/63	
31872	N	2-6-0	SAL	73B	73B	73B	75B	-	05/63	
31873	N	2-6-0	SAL	73B	73B	73B	75A	70C	01/66	
31874	N	2-6-0	EXJ	73B	73B	73B	72A	-	03/64	
31875	N	2-6-0	EXJ	73B	73B	73B	72A	-	08/64	
31876	N1	2-6-0	STL	73C	73C	73C	-	-	11/62	
31877	N1	2-6-0	STL	73C	73C	73C	-	-	10/62	
31878	N1	2-6-0	HIT	73C	73C	73C	-	-	10/62	
31879	N1	2-6-0	HIT	73C	73C	73C	-	-	10/62	
31880	N1	2-6-0	HIT	73C	73C	73C	-	-	11/62	

Number	Class	W.Arrgt.	1948	1952	1955	1959	1963	1966	w/dwn	Notes
31890	U1	2-6-0	BTN	73B	73B	73B	75A	-	06/63	
31891	U1	2-6-0	BTN	73B	73B	73B	75A	-	03/63	
31892	U1	2-6-0	BTN	73A	73C	73E	-	-	11/62	
31893	U1	2-6-0	BTN	73A	73C	73E	-	-	12/62	
31894	U1	2-6-0	BTN	75B	75B	73A	-	-	12/62	
31895	U1	2-6-0	RED	75B	75B	73A	-	-	12/62	
31896	U1	2-6-0	RED	75B	75B	73J	-	-	12/62	
31897	U1	2-6-0	RED	75B	75B	73A	-	-	10/62	
31898	U1	2-6-0	RED	75B	75B	73A	-	-	12/62	
31899	U1	2-6-0	RED	73A	75B	73B	-	-	12/62	
31900	U1	2-6-0	BTN	73A	75A	73B	-	-	12/62	
31901	U1	2-6-0	BA	73A	75A	73B	75A	-	06/63	
31902	U1	2-6-0	BA	73A	75A	73B	-	-	11/62	
31903	U1	2-6-0	BAT	73A	75A	73E	-	-	12/62	
31904	U1	2-6-0	BAT	73A	73A	73A	-	-	11/62	
31905	U1	2-6-0	BAT	73A	73A	73A	-	-	12/62	
31906	U1	2-6-0	BAT	73A	73A	73A	-	-	12/62	
31907	U1	2-6-0	BAT	70A	73A	73A	-	-	12/62	
31908	U1	2-6-0	BAT	70A	74D	73J	-	-	12/62	
31909	U1	2-6-0	BAT	70A	74D	73J	-	-	12/62	
31910	U1	2-6-0	BAT	70A	74D	73J	75A	-	07/63	
31911	W	2-6-4T	HIT	73C	73C	73C	72A	-	10/63	
31912	W	2-6-4T	BAT	73A	73C	73C	72A	-	08/64	
31913	W	2-6-4T	HIT	73C	73C	73C	75C	-	03/64	
31914	W	2-6-4T	BAT	73A	73A	73A	72A	-	08/64	
31915	W	2-6-4T	BAT	73C	73A	73A	72A	-	10/63	
31916	W	2-6-4T	NOR	75C	73C	73C	72A	-	07/63	
31917	W	2-6-4T	NOR	75C	75C	75C	70B	-	01/64	
31918	W	2-6-4T	NOR	75C	75C	75C	75C	-	08/63	
31919	W	2-6-4T	NOR	75C	75C	75C	75C	-	11/63	
31920	W	2-6-4T	NOR	75C	75C	75C	75C	-	07/63	
31921	W	2-6-4T	HIT	73C	73A	73A	75C	-	06/63	
31922	W	2-6-4T	HIT	73C	73C	73C	70B	-	08/63	
31923	W	2-6-4T	HIT	73C	73C	73C	-	-	01/63	
31924	W	2-6-4T	HIT	73C	73C	73C	72A	-	07/64	
31925	W	2-6-4T	HIT	73C	73C	73C	75C	-	11/63	
32001	I1X	4-4-2T	TWW	-	-	-	-	-	07/48	
32002	I1X	4-4-2T	3B	-	-	-	-	-	07/51	
32003	I1X	4-4-2T	TWW	-	-	-	-	-	07/48	
32004	I1X	4-4-2T	TWW	-	-	-	-	-	11/48	
32005	I1X	4-4-2T	EBN	-	-	-	-	-	06/51	
32006	I1X	4-4-2T	TWW	-	-	-	-	-	07/48	
32007	I1X	4-4-2T	3B	-	-	-	-	-	09/48	
32008	I1X	4-4-2T	EBN	-	-	-	-	-	06/51	
32009	I1X	4-4-2T	EBN	-	-	-	-	-	05/51	
32010	I1X	4-4-2T	EBN	-	-	-	-	-	07/48	
32021	I3	4-4-2T	TWW	-	-	-	-	-	10/51	
32022	I3	4-4-2T	TWW	-	-	-	-	-	05/51	
32023	I3	4-4-2T	TWW	-	-	-	-	-	07/51	
32025	I3	4-4-2T	TWW	-	-	-	-	-	01/50	
32026	I3	4-4-2T	TWW	-	-	-	-	-	09/51	
32027	I3	4-4-2T	TWW	-	-	-	-	-	02/51	
32028	I3	4-4-2T	TWW	-	-	-	-	-	10/51	
32029	I3	4-4-2T	TWW	-	-	-	-	-	03/51	
32030	I3	4-4-2T	TWW	-	-	-	-	-	09/51	

Number & Name		Class	W.A.	1948	1952	1955	1959	w/dwn	Notes
32037	Selsey Bill	H1	4-4-2	BTN	-	-	-	07/51	
32038	Portland Bill	H1	4-4-2	BTN	-	-	-	07/51	
32039	Hartland Point	H1	4-4-2	BTN	-	-	-	03/51	

Number	Class	W.Arrgt.	1948	1952	1955	1959	1963	1966	w/dwn	Notes
32043	B4X	4-4-0	BTN	-	-	-	-	-	12/51	
32044	B4	4-4-0	EBN	-	-	-	-	-	09/48	
32045	B4X	4-4-0	HOR	-	-	-	-	-	12/51	
32050	B4X	4-4-0	EBN	-	-	-	-	-	10/51	
32051	B4	4-4-0	HOR	-	-	-	-	-	03/49	
32052	B4X	4-4-0	EBN	-	-	-	-	-	12/51	
32054	B4	4-4-0	EBN	-	-	-	-	-	06/51	
32055	B4X	4-4-0	HOR	-	-	-	-	-	12/51	
32056	B4X	4-4-0	BTN	-	-	-	-	-	11/51	
32060	B4X	4-4-0	BTN	-	-	-	-	-	12/51	
32062	B4	4-4-0	EBN	-	-	-	-	-	05/51	
32063	B4	4-4-0	EBN	-	-	-	-	-	06/51	
32067	B4X	4-4-0	HOR	-	-	-	-	-	10/51	
32068	B4	4-4-0	EBN	-	-	-	-	-	06/51	
32070	B4X	4-4-0	EBN	-	-	-	-	-	09/51	
32071	B4X	4-4-0	BTN	-	-	-	-	-	12/51	
32072	B4X	4-4-0	BTN	-	-	-	-	-	12/51	
32073	B4X	4-4-0	EBN	-	-	-	-	-	09/51	
32074	B4	4-4-0	HOR	-	-	-	-	-	02/50	
32075	I3	4-4-2T	BA	-	-	-	-	-	12/51	
32076	I3	4-4-2T	BA	-	-	-	-	-	12/50	
32077	I3	4-4-2T	BA	-	-	-	-	-	03/51	
32078	I3	4-4-2T	3B	-	-	-	-	-	02/51	
32079	I3	4-4-2T	3B	-	-	-	-	-	11/50	
32080	I3	4-4-2T	3B	-	-	-	-	-	03/50	
32081	I3	4-4-2T	3B	-	-	-	-	-	09/51	
32082	I3	4-4-2T	3B	-	-	-	-	-	06/51	
32083	I3	4-4-2T	EBN	-	-	-	-	-	06/51	
32084	I3	4-4-2T	BTN	-	-	-	-	-	03/51	
32085	I3	4-4-2T	BA	-	-	-	-	-	06/50	
32086	I3	4-4-2T	BTN	-	-	-	-	-	10/51	
32087	I3	4-4-2T	BA	-	-	-	-	-	11/50	
32088	I3	4-4-2T	BTN	-	-	-	-	-	11/50	
32089	I3	4-4-2T	BA	-	-	-	-	-	04/51	
32090	I3	4-4-2T	EBN	-	-	-	-	-	12/50	
32091	I3	4-4-2T	EBN	-	-	-	-	-	06/52	
32094	E1R	0-6-2T	BPL	72D	72D	-	-	-	05/55	
32095	E1R	0-6-2T	BPL	72E	72D	-	-	-	11/56	
32096	E1R	0-6-2T	BPL	72E	72E	-	-	-	11/56	
32097	E1	0-6-0T	BA	-	-	-	-	-	12/49	
32100	E2	0-6-0T	BAT	73A	73A	73A	-	-	11/61	
32101	E2	0-6-0T	BAT	73A	73A	71I	-	-	09/62	
32102	E2	0-6-0T	BAT	73A	73A	73A	-	-	10/61	
32103	E2	0-6-0T	BAT	73A	73A	73A	-	-	10/62	
32104	E2	0-6-0T	BAT	75A	73A	73B	71I	-	04/63	
32105	E2	0-6-0T	BAT	73A	73A	73B	-	-	09/62	
32106	E2	0-6-0T	BAT	75A	73A	73A	-	-	10/62	
32107	E2	0-6-0T	BAT	73A	73A	73B	-	-	02/61	
32108	E2	0-6-0T	DOV	74C	74C	71I	-	-	06/61	
32109	E2	0-6-0T	DOV	74C	74C	71I	71I	-	04/63	
32112	E1	0-6-0T	SOT	-	-	-	-	-	12/49	
32113	E1	0-6-0T	TON	73B	71A	-	-	-	09/58	
32122	E1	0-6-0T	BTN	-	-	-	-	-	05/48	
32124	E1R	0-6-2T	EXJ	72A	72A	72A	-	-	01/59	
32127	E1	0-6-0T	BTN	-	-	-	-	-	12/49	
32128	E1	0-6-0T	BA	-	-	-	-	-	03/52	
32129	E1	0-6-0T	TON	-	-	-	-	-	06/51	
32133	E1	0-6-0T	ELH	71I	-	-	-	-	12/52	
32135	E1R	0-6-2T	EXJ	72A	72A	72A	-	-	02/59	

'Battle of Britain' Class 4-6-2 No. 34074 46 Squadron, with original full height tender. This loco was never rebuilt, and was withdrawn in June 1963 from Exmouth Junction M.P.D., after fifteen years service.

'West Country' Class 4-6-2 No. 34090 Sir Eustace Missenden was named after the last chairman of the Southern Railway, and carried a unique style of nameplate. This loco was new in January 1949, rebuilt in August 1960, and withdrawn in July 1967, after a life of eighteen and a half years.

Number	Class	W.Arrgt.	1948	1952	1955	1959	1963	1966	w/dwn	Notes
32138	E1	0-6-0T	TON	71I	70F	-	-	-	11/56	
32139	E1	0-6-0T	BTN	71D	70F	70F	-	-	01/59	
32141	E1	0-6-0T	BA	-	-	-	-	-	10/49	
32142	E1	0-6-0T	BA	-	-	-	-	-	11/50	
32145	E1	0-6-0T	TON	-	-	-	-	-	06/51	
32147	E1	0-6-0T	ELH	-	-	-	-	-	12/51	
32151	E1	0-6-0T	BA	71A	71A	71I	-	-	01/60	
32153	E1	0-6-0T	FRA	-	-	-	-	-	05/49	
32156	E1	0-6-0T	SOT	-	-	-	-	-	05/51	
32160	E1	0-6-0T	ELH	-	-	-	-	-	12/51	
32162	E1	0-6-0T	SOT	-	-	-	-	-	11/49	
32164	E1	0-6-0T	TON	-	-	-	-	-	06/48	
32165	E3	0-6-2T	BA	73B	75A	75A	-	-	11/59	
32166	E3	0-6-2T	BA	75A	75A	75A	-	-	09/59	
32167	E3	0-6-2T	NOR	75A	75A	-	-	-	10/55	
32168	E3	0-6-2T	BA	75A	70E	-	-	-	01/56	
32169	E3	0-6-2T	NOR	75A	75A	-	-	-	08/55	
32170	E3	0-6-2T	BA	75A	75A	-	-	-	07/57	
32215	D1M	0-4-2T	TWW	-	-	-	-	-	02/50	
32234	D1M	0-4-2T	EBN	-	-	-	-	-	02/50	
32235	D1M	0-4-2T	BTN	-	-	-	-	-	05/49	
32239	D1M	0-4-2T	ELH	-	-	-	-	-	03/48	
32252	D1M	0-4-2T	HOR	-	-	-	-	-	09/50	
32253	D1M	0-4-2T	TWW	-	-	-	-	-	09/49	
32259	D1M	0-4-2T	ELH	-	-	-	-	-	03/48	
32269	D1M	0-4-2T	FRA	-	-	-	-	-	07/48	
32274	D1M	0-4-2T	EBN	-	-	-	-	-	02/50	
32283	D1M	0-4-2T	HOR	-	-	-	-	-	11/48	
32286	D1	0-4-2T	HOR	-	-	-	-	-	07/48	
32289	D1M	0-4-2T	HOR	-	-	-	-	-	07/48	
32299	D1M	0-4-2T	AFD	-	-	-	-	-	05/49	
32300	C3	0-6-0	HOR	-	-	-	-	-	07/51	
32301	C3	0-6-0	HOR	-	-	-	-	-	03/51	
32302	C3	0-6-0	NOR	-	-	-	-	-	01/52	
32303	C3	0-6-0	3B	-	-	-	-	-	10/51	
32306	C3	0-6-0	HOR	-	-	-	-	-	12/51	
32307	C3	0-6-0	HOR	-	-	-	-	-	05/49	
32308	C3	0-6-0	HOR	-	-	-	-	-	11/48	
32309	C3	0-6-0	NOR	-	-	-	-	-	01/49	
32325	J1	4-6-2T	TWW	-	-	-	-	-	06/51	
32326	J2	4-6-2T	TWW	-	-	-	-	-	06/51	

Number & Name		Class	W. A.	1948	1952	1955	1959	1963	1966	w/dwn	Notes
32327	Trevithick	N15X	4-6-0	BAS	70D	70D	-	-	-	01/56	
32328	Hackworth	N15X	4-6-0	BAS	70D	70D	-	-	-	02/55	
32329	Stephenson	N15X	4-6-0	BAS	70D	70D	-	-	-	08/56	
32330	Cudworth	N15X	4-6-0	BAS	70D	70D	-	-	-	08/55	
32331	Beattie	N15X	4-6-0	BAS	70D	70D	-	-	-	07/57	
32332	Stroudley	N15X	4-6-0	BAS	70D	70D	-	-	-	01/56	
32333	Remembrance	N15X	4-6-0	BAS	70D	70D	-	-	-	04/56	

Number	Class	W.Arrgt.	1948	1952	1955	1959	1963	1966	w/dwn	Notes
32337	K	2-6-0	FRA	75A	70F	70F	-	-	12/62	
32338	K	2-6-0	FRA	75A	75A	75A	-	-	12/62	
32339	K	2-6-0	BTN	75A	75A	75A	-	-	11/62	
32340	K	2-6-0	BTN	75A	75A	75A	-	-	12/62	
32341	K	2-6-0	BTN	75A	75A	75A	-	-	12/62	
32342	K	2-6-0	BTN	75A	75A	75A	-	-	12/62	
32343	K	2-6-0	BTN	75A	75A	75A	-	-	12/62	
32344	K	2-6-0	BTN	75A	75E	75E	-	-	11/62	

Number	Class	W.Arrgt.	1948	1952	1955	1959	1963	1966	w/dwn	Notes
32345	K	2-6-0	BTN	75A	75E	75E	-	-	12/62	
32346	K	2-6-0	BTN	75A	75E	75E	-	-	11/62	
32347	K	2-6-0	BTN	75E	75E	75E	-	-	12/62	
32348	K	2-6-0	EBN	75E	75E	75E	-	-	11/62	
32349	K	2-6-0	EBN	71D	70F	70F	-	-	11/62	
32350	K	2-6-0	NOR	75E	75E	75E	-	-	11/62	
32351	K	2-6-0	NOR	75E	75E	75E	-	-	11/62	
32352	K	2-6-0	3B	75E	75E	75E	-	-	11/62	
32353	K	2-6-0	3B	75E	75E	75E	-	-	12/62	
32358	D1M	0-4-2T	EBN	-	-	-	-	-	11/48	
32359	D1	0-4-2T	DOV	-	-	-	-	-	07/51	
32361	D1M	0-4-2T	ELH	-	-	-	-	-	03/48	
32364	D3	0-4-4T	AFD	75D	-	-	-	-	10/52	
32365	D3	0-4-4T	AFD	75A	-	-	-	-	12/52	
32366	D3	0-4-4T	HOR	-	-	-	-	-	03/49	
32367	D3	0-4-4T	TON	-	-	-	-	-	02/49	
32368	D3	0-4-4T	BTN	75A	-	-	-	-	03/53	
32370	D3	0-4-4T	TON	-	-	-	-	-	09/48	
32371	D3	0-4-4T	STL	-	-	-	-	-	10/48	
32372	D3	0-4-4T	BTN	75A	-	-	-	-	05/53	
32373	D3	0-4-4T	HOR	-	-	-	-	-	11/48	
32374	D3	0-4-4T	TON	-	-	-	-	-	02/49	
32376	D3	0-4-4T	BTN	75A	-	-	-	-	05/53	
32377	D3	0-4-4T	EBN	-	-	-	-	-	09/48	
32378	D3	0-4-4T	TON	75A	-	-	-	-	08/52	
32379	D3	0-4-4T	STL	75D	-	-	-	-	12/52	
32380	D3	0-4-4T	AFD	75D	-	-	-	-	05/53	
32383	D3	0-4-4T	STL	-	-	-	-	-	12/48	
32384	D3	0-4-4T	HOR	75G	-	-	-	-	11/53	
32385	D3	0-4-4T	BTN	75G	-	-	-	-	07/53	
32386	D3	0-4-4T	BTN	-	-	-	-	-	06/52	
32387	D3	0-4-4T	HOR	-	-	-	-	-	03/49	
32388	D3	0-4-4T	AFD	-	-	-	-	-	12/51	
32389	D3	0-4-4T	HOR	-	-	-	-	-	03/49	
32390	D3	0-4-4T	TWW	74E	75A	-	-	-	10/55	
32391	D3	0-4-4T	EBN	74E	-	-	-	-	12/52	
32393	D3	0-4-4T	TWW	-	-	-	-	-	10/51	
32394	D3	0-4-4T	STL	-	-	-	-	-	12/51	
32395	D3	0-4-4T	EBN	-	-	-	-	-	06/49	
32397	D3X	0-4-4T	BTN	-	-	-	-	-	07/48	
32398	D3	0-4-4T	TWW	-	-	-	-	-	03/49	
32399	E5	0-6-2T	HOR	75E	-	-	-	-	07/53	
32400	E5	0-6-2T	3B	-	-	-	-	-	12/51	
32401	E5X	0-6-2T	HOR	75A	-	-	-	-	08/54	
32402	E5	0-6-2T	EBN	-	-	-	-	-	03/51	
32404	E5	0-6-2T	NOR	-	-	-	-	-	12/51	
32405	E5	0-6-2T	3B	-	-	-	-	-	12/51	
32406	E5	0-6-2T	EBN	-	-	-	-	-	09/51	
32407	E6X	0-6-2T	NOR	75C	75C	-	-	-	11/57	
32408	E6	0-6-2T	BA	73B	73B	73B	-	-	12/62	
32409	E6	0-6-2T	ELH	73B	73B	-	-	-	01/58	
32410	E6	0-6-2T	BA	73B	73B	73B	-	-	06/61	
32411	E6X	0-6-2T	NOR	75C	75C	75C	-	-	02/59	
32412	E6	0-6-2T	BA	71A	73B	-	-	-	09/57	
32413	E6	0-6-2T	BA	71A	75C	75C	-	-	02/58	
32414	E6	0-6-2T	NOR	75C	75C	-	-	-	06/58	
32415	E6	0-6-2T	BA	73B	73B	73B	-	-	09/61	
32416	E6	0-6-2T	NOR	71A	75C	75C	-	-	02/62	

Number	Class	W.Arrgt.	1948	1952	1955	1959	1963	1966	w/dwn	Notes
32417	E6	0-6-2T	NOR	75C	75C	73B	-	-	12/62	
32418	E6	0-6-2T	NOR	75C	75C	73B	-	-	12/62	

Number & Name		Class	W. A.	1948	1952	1955	1959	1963	1966	w/dwn	Notes
32421	South Foreland	H2	4-4-2	NHN	75A	75A	-	-	-	08/56	
32422	North Foreland	H2	4-4-2	NHN	75A	75A	-	-	-	10/56	
32423	The Needles	H2	4-4-2	NHN	-	-	-	-	-	05/49	
32424	Beachy Head	H2	4-4-2	NHN	75A	75A	-	-	-	04/58	
32425	Trevose Head	H2	4-4-2	NHN	75A	75A	-	-	-	10/56	
32426	St. Alban's Head	H2	4-4-2	NHN	75A	75A	-	-	-	08/56	

Number	Class	W.Arrgt.	1948	1952	1955	1959	1963	1966	w/dwn	Notes
32434	C2X	0-6-0	NHN	75A	75A	-	-	-	03/57	
32435	C2	0-6-0	RED	-	-	-	-	-	05/48	
32436	C2	0-6-0	3B	-	-	-	-	-	01/50	
32437	C2X	0-6-0	BTN	75A	75A	70B	-	-	06/59	
32438	C2X	0-6-0	BTN	75A	75A	70B	-	-	12/61	
32440	C2X	0-6-0	NOR	75A	75A	-	-	-	10/58	
32441	C2X	0-6-0	3B	75A	75A	75A	-	-	10/61	
32442	C2X	0-6-0	BA	75A	75A	75A	-	-	03/60	
32443	C2X	0-6-0	BTN	75C	75C	75C	-	-	09/60	
32444	C2X	0-6-0	NOR	75C	75C	75C	-	-	03/60	
32445	C2X	0-6-0	3B	75C	75C	75C	-	-	11/61	
32446	C2X	0-6-0	BA	75C	75C	75C	-	-	11/60	
32447	C2X	0-6-0	NOR	75C	75C	75C	-	-	02/60	
32448	C2X	0-6-0	BA	75B	75B	75C	-	-	10/61	
32449	C2X	0-6-0	HOR	75B	75B	75A	-	-	06/61	
32450	C2X	0-6-0	RED	75B	75B	75B	-	-	10/61	
32451	C2X	0-6-0	3B	75B	75B	75B	-	-	11/61	
32453	E3	0-6-2T	BA	73B	73B	-	-	-	08/55	
32454	E3	0-6-2T	BA	74D	74D	-	-	-	03/58	
32455	E3	0-6-2T	NOR	73B	73A	-	-	-	02/58	
32456	E3	0-6-2T	NOR	74D	74D	73J	-	-	08/59	
32457	E3	0-6-2T	NOR	-	-	-	-	-	05/49	
32458	E3	0-6-2T	BA	73B	73B	-	-	-	03/57	
32459	E3	0-6-2T	BA	73B	73B	-	-	-	06/56	
32460	E3	0-6-2T	BA	73B	73B	-	-	-	04/56	
32461	E3	0-6-2T	BA	73B	73B	-	-	-	04/57	
32462	E3	0-6-2T	BA	73B	73B	-	-	-	05/57	
32463	E4	0-6-2T	BA	75D	75D	75D	-	-	09/59	
32464	E4	0-6-2T	HOR	75D	75D	-	-	-	02/56	
32465	E4	0-6-2T	3B	75D	75D	-	-	-	04/55	
32466	E4X	0-6-2T	NOR	75C	75C	75C	-	-	12/58	
32467	E4	0-6-2T	BA	75D	75D	-	-	-	04/58	
32468	E4	0-6-2T	BA	75D	75D	75A	-	-	01/63	
32469	E4	0-6-2T	BA	75D	75D	75D	-	-	10/61	
32470	E4	0-6-2T	BTN	75D	75D	75D	-	-	06/62	
32471	E4	0-6-2T	BTN	73B	73B	73B	-	-	09/59	
32472	E4	0-6-2T	BA	73B	73B	73B	-	-	06/62	
32473	E4	0-6-2T	NOR	73B	73B	73B	-	-	11/62	
32474	E4	0-6-2T	BA	73B	73B	73B	75A	-	05/63	
32475	E4	0-6-2T	NHN	75A	75A	75A	-	-	06/61	
32476	E4	0-6-2T	NOR	75C	70A	-	-	-	04/57	
32477	E4X	0-6-2T	NOR	75C	75C	75C	-	-	01/59	
32478	E4X	0-6-2T	NOR	75C	75C	-	-	-	08/56	
32479	E4	0-6-2T	NOR	71D	70F	70F	75A	-	06/63	
32480	E4	0-6-2T	3B	75E	75E	75A	-	-	11/59	
32481	E4	0-6-2T	NOR	75E	75E	-	-	-	04/58	
32482	E4	0-6-2T	NHN	75B	75A	-	-	-	11/55	

Number	Class	W.Arrgt.	1948	1952	1955	1959	1963	1966	w/dwn	Notes
32484	E4	0-6-2T	3B	75E	75C	75A	-	-	09/60	
32485	E4	0-6-2T	EBN	75G	75A	-	-	-	12/57	
32486	E4	0-6-2T	BTN	72B	72B	70A	-	-	01/59	
32487	E4	0-6-2T	GFD	70C	70C	70A	-	-	12/62	
32488	E4	0-6-2T	TON	74D	74D	-	-	-	06/57	
32489	E4X	0-6-2T	NOR	75C	75C	-	-	-	05/55	
32490	E4	0-6-2T	FRA	70C	70C	-	-	-	12/55	
32491	E4	0-6-2T	BTN	71A	71A	71A	-	-	01/61	
32492	E4	0-6-2T	NHN	71A	71A	-	-	-	05/57	
32493	E4	0-6-2T	NOR	70A	70A	-	-	-	02/58	
32494	E4	0-6-2T	NHN	75A	75A	75A	-	-	09/59	
32495	E4	0-6-2T	NOR	71D	70F	70F	-	-	09/60	
32496	E4	0-6-2T	HOR	75A	75A	-	-	-	11/55	
32497	E4	0-6-2T	3B	70A	70A	70A	-	-	11/59	
32498	E4	0-6-2T	NOR	70A	70A	70A	-	-	11/61	
32499	E4	0-6-2T	NHN	70A	70A	-	-	-	06/57	
32500	E4	0-6-2T	GFD	70A	70A	70A	-	-	01/62	
32501	E4	0-6-2T	HOR	70E	70E	-	-	-	08/55	
32502	E4	0-6-2T	NOR	70E	70E	-	-	-	02/58	
32503	E4	0-6-2T	TON	74D	74D	75A	75A	-	04/63	
32504	E4	0-6-2T	GFD	75A	75A	75A	-	-	11/61	
32505	E4	0-6-2T	BTN	71D	70F	70C	-	-	03/61	
32506	E4	0-6-2T	NOR	72B	72B	70C	-	-	06/61	
32507	E4	0-6-2T	RED	75B	75B	75A	-	-	04/59	
32508	E4	0-6-2T	NHN	75A	75A	75A	-	-	01/60	
32509	E4	0-6-2T	FRA	71D	70F	70F	-	-	03/62	
32510	E4	0-6-2T	ELH	71A	71A	71A	-	-	09/62	
32511	E4	0-6-2T	HOR	75A	75A	-	-	-	10/56	
32512	E4	0-6-2T	TWW	75B	75B	75A	-	-	05/61	
32513	E4	0-6-2T	BTN	75A	75A	-	-	-	01/56	
32514	E4	0-6-2T	BTN	75A	75A	-	-	-	10/56	
32515	E4	0-6-2T	HOR	75A	75A	75A	-	-	05/61	
32516	E4	0-6-2T	3B	75E	75E	-	-	-	10/55	
32517	E4	0-6-2T	RED	75G	75F	75F	-	-	06/59	
32518	E4	0-6-2T	EBN	75G	75A	-	-	-	06/55	
32519	E4	0-6-2T	3B	75E	75E	75A	-	-	09/59	
32520	E4	0-6-2T	3B	75E	75E	-	-	-	01/57	
32521	C2X	0-6-0	HOR	75D	75D	75C	-	-	12/61	
32522	C2X	0-6-0	3B	75D	75D	75D	-	-	10/61	
32523	C2X	0-6-0	BTN	75D	75D	75E	-	-	02/62	
32524	C2X	0-6-0	BA	73B	73B	-	-	-	02/58	
32525	C2X	0-6-0	BA	73B	73B	73B	-	-	01/62	
32526	C2X	0-6-0	NOR	75E	73B	75D	-	-	02/60	
32527	C2X	0-6-0	3B	75E	73B	75E	-	-	11/60	
32528	C2X	0-6-0	BTN	75E	75E	75E	-	-	03/61	
32529	C2X	0-6-0	3B	75E	75E	75E	-	-	10/59	
32532	C2X	0-6-0	3B	75E	75E	75E	-	-	06/60	
32533	C2	0-6-0	NHN	-	-	-	-	-	02/50	
32534	C2X	0-6-0	NHN	75E	75E	75E	-	-	10/61	
32535	C2X	0-6-0	NOR	75E	75E	75E	-	-	02/62	
32536	C2X	0-6-0	NOR	75E	75E	75E	-	-	03/61	
32537	C2X	0-6-0	FRA	75E	75E	-	-	-	04/57	
32538	C2X	0-6-0	EBN	75G	75E	73B	-	-	12/61	
32539	C2X	0-6-0	BTN	75A	75A	73B	-	-	11/61	
32540	C2X	0-6-0	NOR	75A	75A	-	-	-	03/58	
32541	C2X	0-6-0	RED	75G	75D	75D	-	-	02/61	
32543	C2X	0-6-0	BTN	75G	75C	73A	-	-	09/60	
32544	C2X	0-6-0	NOR	75C	75C	75C	-	-	11/61	
32545	C2X	0-6-0	3B	75C	75C	75C	-	-	12/61	

Number	Class	W.Arrgt.	1948	1952	1955	1959	1963	1966	w/dwn	Notes
32546	C2X	0-6-0	BTN	75C	75C	75C	-	-	04/61	
32547	C2X	0-6-0	NOR	75C	75C	73A	-	-	11/61	
32548	C2X	0-6-0	FRA	71D	70F	70F	-	-	11/61	
32549	C2X	0-6-0	BA	71D	70F	70F	-	-	11/61	
32550	C2X	0-6-0	HOR	71D	70F	70F	-	-	12/61	
32551	C2X	0-6-0	BA	73B	73B	73B	-	-	02/60	
32552	C2X	0-6-0	3B	75E	73B	73B	-	-	06/61	
32553	C2X	0-6-0	3B	75E	73B	73B	-	-	08/61	
32554	C2X	0-6-0	FRA	73B	73B	73B	-	-	02/60	
32556	E4	0-6-2T	HOR	71A	71A	71A	-	-	09/61	
32557	E4	0-6-2T	HOR	71A	71A	73B	-	-	12/62	
32558	E4	0-6-2T	BTN	71A	71A	-	-	-	11/56	
32559	E4	0-6-2T	FRA	71A	71A	71A	-	-	06/60	
32560	E4	0-6-2T	RED	75B	75B	-	-	-	08/58	
32561	E4	0-6-2T	NOR	75B	75B	-	-	-	06/56	
32562	E4	0-6-2T	FRA	71A	71A	75A	-	-	08/60	
32563	E4	0-6-2T	NOR	71A	71A	70A	-	-	08/61	
32564	E4	0-6-2T	BA	73B	73B	73B	-	-	09/61	
32565	E4	0-6-2T	BA	73B	73B	73B	-	-	06/61	
32566	E4	0-6-2T	BTN	75A	75A	75A	-	-	04/59	
32567	E5	0-6-2T	BTNR	-	-	-	-	-	11/49	
32568	E5	0-6-2T	ED	71D	70D	-	-	-	02/55	
32570	E5X	0-6-2T	HOR	75D	75D	-	-	-	01/56	
32571	E5	0-6-2T	HOR	75E	75C	-	-	-	01/56	
32572	E5	0-6-2T	3B	-	-	-	-	-	03/49	
32573	E5	0-6-2T	HOR	75A	-	-	-	-	08/53	
32574	E5	0-6-2T	EBN	-	-	-	-	-	06/51	
32575	E5	0-6-2T	EBN	-	-	-	-	-	12/51	
32576	E5X	0-6-2T	BTN	75D	75D	-	-	-	07/55	
32577	E4	0-6-2T	BTN	75A	75A	75A	-	-	10/59	
32578	E4	0-6-2T	BA	74D	74E	73J	-	-	04/61	
32579	E4	0-6-2T	NOR	71A	71A	71A	-	-	11/59	
32580	E4	0-6-2T	TON	74D	74D	73J	-	-	04/62	
32581	E4	0-6-2T	TWW	75F	75F	75F	-	-	04/62	
32582	E4	0-6-2T	TWW	75D	75F	-	-	-	10/56	
32583	E5	0-6-2T	BTN	75A	70D	-	-	-	01/56	
32584	E5	0-6-2T	HOR	-	-	-	-	-	02/51	
32585	E5	0-6-2T	3B	75G	-	-	-	-	06/54	
32586	E5X	0-6-2T	RED	75A	75A	-	-	-	04/55	
32587	E5	0-6-2T	BTN	75F	-	-	-	-	11/54	
32588	E5	0-6-2T	EBN	75G	-	-	-	-	12/53	
32589	E5	0-6-2T	TWW	-	-	-	-	-	01/49	
32590	E5	0-6-2T	TWW	-	-	-	-	-	09/51	
32591	E5	0-6-2T	TWW	70D	-	-	-	-	12/54	
32592	E5	0-6-2T	RED	70D	-	-	-	-	05/53	
32593	E5	0-6-2T	3B	74C	74C	-	-	-	01/56	
32594	E5	0-6-2T	HOR	-	-	-	-	-	03/51	
32595	I1X	4-4-2T	EBN	-	-	-	-	-	06/51	
32596	I1X	4-4-2T	EBN	-	-	-	-	-	06/51	
32598	I1X	4-4-2T	3B	-	-	-	-	-	07/48	
32599	I1X	4-4-2T	3B	-	-	-	-	-	09/48	
32601	I1X	4-4-2T	3B	-	-	-	-	-	02/48	
32602	I1X	4-4-2T	3B	-	-	-	-	-	06/51	
32603	I1X	4-4-2T	TWW	-	-	-	-	-	04/51	
32604	I1X	4-4-2T	3B	-	-	-	-	-	09/48	
32605	D1M	0-4-2T	EBN	-	-	-	-	-	11/48	
32606	E1	0-6-0T	BTN	71I	71I	-	-	-	08/56	
32608	E1R	0-6-2T	BPL	72E	72E	-	-	-	05/57	
32609	E1	0-6-0T	ELH	72E	-	-	-	-	06/48	

Page 64

*'West Country' 4-6-2 No. 34100 Appledore was one of this class which didn't have a
shield with the city or county Coat of Arms mounted above the nameplate.
Withdrawn during July 1967 from Salisbury M.P.D (70E)*

*One of the delightful 'O2' class 0-4-4Ts on the Isle of Wight system, No. W22 Brading,
resting in the summer sun while nursing a burned smokebox and chimney.*

*Almost at the end of steam, it was proposed to use redundant B.R. Standard 2MT
2-6-2Ts to replace the 'O2's, but at the last minute the scheme was abandoned in
favour of electrification using ex - London Transport 'tube' stock.*

Number	Class	W.Arrgt.	1948	1952	1955	1959	1963	1966	w/dwn	Notes
32610	E1R	0-6-2T	BPL	72E	72E	-	-	-	04/56	
32635	A1X	0-6-0T	-	-	-	-	75A	-	03/63	Renumbered from DS377 03/59
32636	A1X	0-6-0T	NHN	75A	75A	73F	75A	-	11/63	
32640	A1X	0-6-0T	FRA	75A	70F	70F	71A	-	09/63	
32644	A1X	0-6-0T	FRA	-	-	-	-	-	04/51	
32646	A1X	0-6-0T	-	75A	75A	70F	71A	-	11/63	Renumbered from W8 09/49
32647	A1X	0-6-0T	NHN	-	-	-	-	-	10/51	
32650	A1X	0-6-0T	-	-	70F	70F	71A	-	11/63	Renumbered from DS515 11/53
32655	A1X	0-6-0T	FRA	71D	74E	75A	-	-	05/60	
32659	A1X	0-6-0T	FRA	74A	-	-	-	-	08/53	
32661	A1X	0-6-0T	FRA	71D	70F	70F	71A	-	04/63	
32662	A1X	0-6-0T	FRA	71D	75A	75A	75A	-	11/63	
32670	A1X	0-6-0T	KESR	74A	74E	75A	75A	-	11/63	
32677	A1X	0-6-0T	-	74A	70F	70F	-	-	09/59	originally K.E.S.R. No. 3
32678	A1X	0-6-0T	-	74A	74E	70F	71A	-	10/63	Renumbered from W13 09/49
32689	E1	0-6-0T	SOT	71I	71I	71I	-	-	02/60	
32690	E1	0-6-0T	FRA	-	-	-	-	-	01/50	
32691	E1	0-6-0T	FRA	-	-	-	-	-	12/51	
32694	E1	0-6-0T	FRA	71D	70F	70F	-	-	07/61	
32695	E1R	0-6-2T	EXJ	72A	72A	-	-	-	04/57	
32696	E1R	0-6-2T	BPL	72E	72E	-	-	-	01/56	
32697	E1R	0-6-2T	EXJ	72A	72A	72A	-	-	11/59	
32699	D1M	0-4-2T	ELH	-	-	-	-	-	02/48	
33001	Q1	0-6-0	GFD	70C	70C	70C	70B	-	05/64	
33002	Q1	0-6-0	GFD	70C	70C	70C	70B	-	07/63	
33003	Q1	0-6-0	GFD	70C	70C	70C	70B	-	06/64	
33004	Q1	0-6-0	GFD	70C	70C	70C	70B	-	01/65	
33005	Q1	0-6-0	GFD	70C	70C	70C	70B	-	06/63	
33006	Q1	0-6-0	GFD	70B	70B	70B	70B	70C	01/66	
33007	Q1	0-6-0	GFD	70B	70B	70B	70B	-	01/64	
33008	Q1	0-6-0	GFD	70B	70B	70B	70B	-	08/63	
33009	Q1	0-6-0	GFD	70B	70B	70B	70B	-	09/65	
33010	Q1	0-6-0	GFD	70B	70B	70B	70B	-	01/64	
33011	Q1	0-6-0	GFD	70B	70B	70B	70B	-	08/63	
33012	Q1	0-6-0	GFD	70B	70B	70B	70B	-	11/64	
33013	Q1	0-6-0	GFD	70B	70B	70B	70B	-	07/63	
33014	Q1	0-6-0	ELH	73C	73C	73C	75E	-	01/64	
33015	Q1	0-6-0	ELH	73C	73A	70A	75E	-	11/64	
33016	Q1	0-6-0	ELH	71A	70B	70B	75E	-	08/63	
33017	Q1	0-6-0	ELH	71A	73A	70A	75E	-	01/64	
33018	Q1	0-6-0	ELH	71A	70B	70B	75E	-	07/65	
33019	Q1	0-6-0	ELH	71A	70C	70C	70C	-	12/63	
33020	Q1	0-6-0	ELH	71A	71A	71A	71A	70C	01/66	
33021	Q1	0-6-0	ELH	71A	71A	71A	71A	-	08/63	
33022	Q1	0-6-0	ELH	71A	70C	70C	70C	-	01/64	
33023	Q1	0-6-0	ELH	71A	71A	71A	71A	-	06/64	
33024	Q1	0-6-0	ELH	71A	74D	73J	75E	-	08/63	
33025	Q1	0-6-0	ELH	71A	70C	70C	70C	-	07/63	
33026	Q1	0-6-0	TON	74D	70B	70B	75E	-	09/65	
33027	Q1	0-6-0	TON	74D	70B	70B	70B	70C	01/66	
33028	Q1	0-6-0	TON	74D	74D	73J	-	-	02/63	
33029	Q1	0-6-0	TON	74D	74D	73J	75E	-	01/64	
33030	Q1	0-6-0	TON	74D	74D	73J	75E	-	06/64	
33031	Q1	0-6-0	FEL	74D	74D	73J	75E	-	09/63	
33032	Q1	0-6-0	FEL	74D	74D	73J	70C	-	01/64	
33033	Q1	0-6-0	FEL	74D	74D	73J	70C	-	06/64	
33034	Q1	0-6-0	FEL	74D	74D	73J	70C	-	01/64	
33035	Q1	0-6-0	FEL	74D	74D	73J	70C	-	06/64	
33036	Q1	0-6-0	FEL	73A	74D	73J	70C	-	06/64	

Class E1 0-6-0T No.W3 Ryde was one of four E1s which were used for freight and Engineers' trains, and was taken out of service during July 1959. The Isle of Wight system was completely self contained, and had full carriage, wagon, and loco repair facilities.

Taken on the same day as No. W22 (see page 65), and just ahead of it, is O2 Class No.W36 Carisbrooke, which, along with No.W35 Freshwater came to the island in 1949, just shortly after Nationalisation, in exchange for the two remaining Class A1X

Number	Class	W.Arrgt.	1948	1952	1955	1959	1963	1966	w/dwn	Notes
33037	Q1	0-6-0	FEL	73A	73C	73C	71A	-	10/63	
33038	Q1	0-6-0	FEL	73A	73A	70A	70B	-	01/64	
33039	Q1	0-6-0	FEL	74E	74E	73C	71A	-	06/64	
33040	Q1	0-6-0	FEL	74E	74E	73C	70B	-	06/64	

Number & Name	Class	W. A.	1948	1952	1955	1959	1963	1966	w/dwn	Notes
34001 Exeter	WC	4-6-2	EXJ	72A	72A	73B	70A	70A	07/67	Rbt. 11/57
34002 Salisbury	WC	4-6-2	EXJ	72A	72A	72A	72A	70A	04/67	
34003 Plymouth	WC	4-6-2	EXJ	72A	72A	73B	70E	-	09/64	Rbt. 09/57
34004 Yeovil	WC	4-6-2	EXJ	72A	72A	73B	71A	70F	07/67	Rbt. 02/58
34005 Barnstaple	WC	4-6-2	EXJ	70A	70A	73B	70E	70F	10/66	Rbt. 06/57
34006 Bude	WC	4-6-2	EXJ	70A	70A	70A	70A	70E	03/67	
34007 Wadebridge	WC	4-6-2	EXJ	70A	70A	70A	70A	-	10/65	
34008 Padstow	WC	4-6-2	EXJ	70A	70A	75A	71A	70D	06/67	Rbt. 07/60
34009 Lyme Regis	WC	4-6-2	EXJ	70A	70A	70A	70A	70D	10/66	Rbt. 01/61
34010 Sidmouth	WC	4-6-2	EXJ	70A	70A	70A	70A	-	03/65	Rbt. 02/59
34011 Tavistock	WC	4-6-2	EXJ	70A	70A	70A	72A	-	11/63	
34012 Launceston	WC	4-6-2	EXJ	70A	70A	73B	75A	70F	12/66	Rbt. 01/58
34013 Okehampton	WC	4-6-2	EXJ	72A	72A	73B	75A	70E	07/67	Rbt. 10/57
34014 Budleigh Saltern	WC	4-6-2	EXJ	72A	72A	73B	75A	-	03/65	Rbt. 03/58
34015 Exmouth	WC	4-6-2	EXJ	72A	72A	72A	72A	70E	04/67	
34016 Bodmin	WC	4-6-2	EXJ	72A	72A	73G	71A	-	06/64	Rbt. 04/58
34017 Ilfracombe	WC	4-6-2	EXJ	70A	73A	73G	70A	70D	10/66	Rbt. 11/57
34018 Axminster	WC	4-6-2	EXJ	70A	70A	70A	70A	70D	07/67	Rbt. 10/58
34019 Bideford	WC	4-6-2	EXJ	70A	70A	75A	75A	70D	03/67	
34020 Seaton	WC	4-6-2	EXJ	70A	70A	70A	72A	-	09/64	
34021 Dartmoor	WC	4-6-2	EXJ	72A	72A	73G	71A	70A	07/67	Rbt. 01/58
34022 Exmoor	WC	4-6-2	9E	72A	72A	73G	71A	-	04/65	Rbt. 12/57
34023 Blackmoor Vale	WC	4-6-2	9E	72A	72A	72A	72A	70D	07/67	
34024 Tamar Valley	WC	4-6-2	EXJ	72A	72A	72A	72A	70F	07/67	Rbt. 02/61
34025 Whimple	WC	4-6-2	EXJ	72A	72A	73G	71A	70F	07/67	Rbt. 11/57
34026 Yes Tor	WC	4-6-2	EXJ	72A	72A	73G	70E	70E	09/66	Rbt. 02/58
34027 Taw Valley	WC	4-6-2	EXJ	72A	72A	73G	75A	-	08/64	Rbt. 09/57
34028 Eddystone	WC	4-6-2	EXJ	72A	72A	72A	71A	-	05/64	Rbt. 08/58
34029 Lundy	WC	4-6-2	EXJ	72A	72A	72A	71B	-	09/64	Rbt. 12/58
34030 Watersmeet	WC	4-6-2	RAM	72A	72A	72A	72A	-	09/64	
34031 Torrington	WC	4-6-2	RAM	72A	72A	72A	70A	-	02/65	Rbt. 12/58
34032 Camelford	WC	4-6-2	RAM	72A	72A	72A	72A	70D	10/66	Rbt. 10/60
34033 Chard	WC	4-6-2	BAT	72A	72A	72A	72A	-	12/65	
34034 Honiton	WC	4-6-2	BAT	72A	72A	72A	71A	70D	07/67	Rbt. 08/60
34035 Shaftesbury	WC	4-6-2	BAT	72D	72D	72A	72A	-	06/63	
34036 Westward Ho	WC	4-6-2	BAT	72D	72D	72A	72A	70D	07/67	Rbt. 09/60
34037 Clovelly	WC	4-6-2	BAT	72D	72D	73G	71A	70D	07/67	Rbt. 03/58
34038 Lynton	WC	4-6-2	BAT	72D	72D	72A	71A	70A	06/66	
34039 Boscastle	WC	4-6-2	BAT	30A	75A	75A	71A	-	05/65	Rbt. 01/59
34040 Crewkerne	WC	4-6-2	BAT	71G	71A	71B	71B	70F	07/67	Rbt. 10/60
34041 Wilton	WC	4-6-2	EXJ	71G	71A	71B	71B	70D	01/66	
34042 Dorchester	WC	4-6-2	EXJ	71G	71A	71B	71B	-	10/65	Rbt. 01/59
34043 Coombe Martin	WC	4-6-2	EXJ	71B	71B	71B	71B	-	06/63	
34044 Woolacombe	WC	4-6-2	EXJ	71B	71B	71B	71B	70F	05/67	Rbt. 05/60
34045 Ottery St. Mary	WC	4-6-2	EXJ	75A	75A	70A	71B	-	06/64	Rbt. 10/58
34046 Braunton	WC	4-6-2	EXJ	75A	75A	75A	71B	-	10/65	Rbt. 02/59
34047 Callington	WC	4-6-2	EXJ	75A	75A	70A	71B	70F	06/67	Rbt. 10/58
34048 Crediton	WC	4-6-2	SAL	75A	75A	75A	70E	70E	03/66	Rbt. 03/59
34049 Anti Aircraft Command	BB	4-6-2	SAL	72B	72B	72B	70E	-	11/63	
34050 Royal Observer Corps	BB	4-6-2	SAL	72B	72B	72B	70A	-	08/65	Rbt. 08/58
34051 Winston Churchill	BB	4-6-2	SAL	72B	72B	72B	70E	-	09/65	
34052 Lord Dowding	BB	4-6-2	SAL	72B	72B	72B	70E	70E	07/67	Rbt. 09/58
34053 Sir Keith Park	BB	4-6-2	SAL	72B	72B	72B	71B	-	10/65	Rbt. 11/58
34054 Lord Beaverbrook	BB	4-6-2	BAT	72B	72B	72B	70E	-	09/64	

Class Q1 0-6-0 No. 33014 was one of Bulleid's unconventional austerity locos built for war service on the Southern Railway during the early 1940s.

They may have looked strange with no footplate and tunnel shaped three part boiler casing, but they were very powerful, and eliminated a lot of double heading on heavy trains.

Class A1 0-6-0T DS680 was the last 'Terrier' not to be rebuilt to A1X specification with extended smokebox, and was a works shunter at Lancing Carriage Works until June 1962.

Number & Name	Class	W.A.	1948	1952	1955	1959	1963	1966	w/dwn	Notes
34055 Fighter Pilot	BB	4-6-2	BAT	72B	72B	72B	75A	-	06/63	
34056 Croydon	BB	4-6-2	DOV	72A	72A	72A	72A	70E	05/67	Rbt. 12/60
34057 Biggin Hill	BB	4-6-2	DOV	72A	72A	72A	75A	70E	05/67	
34058 Sir Frederick Pile	BB	4-6-2	9E	72A	72A	72A	72A	-	10/64	Rbt. 11/60
34059 Sir Archibald Sinclair	BB	4-6-2	9E	72A	72A	72B	70E	70E	05/66	Rbt. 03/60
34060 25 Squadron	BB	4-6-2	9E	72A	72A	72A	72A	70D	07/67	Rbt. 11/60
34061 73 Squadron	BB	4-6-2	9E	72A	72A	72A	71A	-	08/64	
34062 17 Squadron	BB	4-6-2	RAM	72A	72A	72A	72A	-	06/64	Rbt. 04/59
34063 229 Squadron	BB	4-6-2	RAM	70A	70A	70A	72A	-	08/65	
34064 Fighter Command	BB	4-6-2	9E	70A	70A	70A	70A	70E	05/66	
34065 Hurricane	BB	4-6-2	RAM	70A	73A	70A	72A	-	04/64	
34066 Spitfire	BB	4-6-2	RAM	73A	73A	73A	72A	70E	09/66	
34067 Tangmere	BB	4-6-2	RAM	73A	73A	73A	70E	-	11/63	
34068 Kenley	BB	4-6-2	RAM	73A	73A	73A	70E	-	12/63	
34069 Hawkinge	BB	4-6-2	RAM	73A	72A	72A	72A	-	11/63	
34070 Manston	BB	4-6-2	RAM	73A	73A	73H	72A	-	08/64	
34071 601 Squadron	BB	4-6-2	04/48	73A	73A	73H	70A	70D	04/67	Rbt. 05/60
34072 257 Squadron	BB	4-6-2	04/48	74C	74C	72A	72A	-	10/64	
34073 249 Squadron	BB	4-6-2	05/48	74C	74C	73H	70A	-	06/64	
34074 46 Squadron	BB	4-6-2	05/48	74C	74C	72A	72A	-	06/63	
34075 264 Squadron	BB	4-6-2	06/48	74B	74B	72A	72A	-	04/64	
34076 41 Squadron	BB	4-6-2	06/48	74B	74B	72A	72A	70E	01/66	
34077 603 Squadron	BB	4-6-2	07/48	74B	74B	73A	70A	70D	03/67	Rbt. 07/60
34078 222 Squadron	BB	4-6-2	07/48	74B	74B	73G	72A	-	09/64	
34079 141 Squadron	BB	4-6-2	07/48	74B	74B	72A	72A	70D	02/66	
34080 74 Squadron	BB	4-6-2	08/48	74B	74B	72A	72A	-	09/64	
34081 92 Squadron	BB	4-6-2	09/48	74B	74B	72A	72A	-	08/64	
34082 615 Squadron	BB	4-6-2	09/48	74B	74B	73H	70A	70D	04/66	Rbt. 04/60
34083 605 Squadron	BB	4-6-2	10/48	74B	74B	73H	72A	-.	07/64	
34084 253 Squadron	BB	4-6-2	11/48	74B	74B	73H	72A	-	10/65	
34085 501 Squadron	BB	4-6-2	11/48	74B	74B	73A	71B	-	09/65	Rbt. 06/60
34086 219 Squadron	BB	4-6-2	12/48	74B	74B	73A	72A	70D	06/66	
34087 145 Squadron	BB	4-6-2	12/48	73A	73A	73A	70A	70D	07/67	Rbt. 12/60
34088 213 Squadron	BB	4-6-2	12/48	73A	73A	73A	70A	70D	03/67	Rbt. 04/60
34089 602 Squadron	BB	4-6-2	12/48	30A	73A	73A	75A	70E	07/67	Rbt. 11/60
34090 Sir Eustace Missenden, Southern Railway	BB	4-6-2	01/49	73A	73A	70A	70A	70D	07/67	Rbt. 08/60
34091 Weymouth	WC	4-6-2	09/49	73A	73A	73A	70E	-	09/64	
34092 City of Wells	WC	4-6-2	09/49	73A	73A	73A	70E	-	11/64	
34093 Saunton	WC	4-6-2	10/49	71B	71B	70A	70A	70D	07/67	Rbt. 05/60
34094 Mortehoe	WC	4-6-2	10/49	71B	71B	70A	70A	-	08/64	
34095 Brentor	WC	4-6-2	10/49	71B	71B	70A	70A	70D	07/67	Rbt. 01/61
34096 Trevone	WC	4-6-2	11/49	74B	74B	72A	72A	-	09/64	Rbt. 04/61
34097 Holsworthy	WC	4-6-2	11/49	74B	74B	71B	71A	70D	04/66	Rbt. 03/61
34098 Templecombe	WC	4-6-2	12/49	74B	74B	71B	71A	70D	06/67	Rbt. 02/61
34099 Lynmouth	WC	4-6-2	12/49	74B	74B	71B	70E	-	11/64	
34100 Appledore	WC	4-6-2	12/49	74B	74B	73A	75A	70E	07/67	Rbt. 09/60
34101 Hartland	WC	4-6-2	02/50	73A	73A	73A	75A	70D	07/66	Rbt. 09/60
34102 Lapford	WC	4-6-2	03/50	73A	73A	71B	71B	70D	07/67	
34103 Calstock	WC	4-6-2	02/50	73A	73A	73H	71B	-	09/65	
34104 Bere Alston	WC	4-6-2	04/50	73A	73A	72A	71A	70D	06/67	Rbt. 05/61
34105 Swanage	WC	4-6-2	03/50	71B	71B	71B	71B	-	10/64	
34106 Lydford	WC	4-6-2	03/50	71B	71B	72A	72A	-	09/64	
34107 Blandford Forum	WC	4-6-2	04/50	71B	71B	71B	72A	-	09/64	
34108 Wincanton	WC	4-6-2	04/50	71B	71B	72A	72A	70E	06/67	Rbt. 05/61
34109 Sir Trafford Leigh Mallory	BB	4-6-2	05/50	71B	71B	72A	72A	-	09/64	Rbt. 03/61
34110 66 Squadron	BB	4-6-2	01/51	71B	71B	71B	72A	-	11/63	

Number & Name	Class	W. A.	1948	1952	1955	1959	1963	1966	w/dwn	Notes
35001 Channel Packet	MN	4-6-2	EXJ	72A	72A	73A	70A	-	11/64	Rbt. 08/59
35002 Union Castle	MN	4-6-2	EXJ	72A	72A	71B	71B	-	02/64	Rbt. 05/58
35003 Royal Mail	MN	4-6-2	EXJ	72A	72A	72A	72A	70F	07/67	Rbt. 09/59
35004 Cunard White Star	MN	4-6-2	EXJ	72A	72A	72B	70E	-	10/65	Rbt. 07/58
35005 Canadian Pacific	MN	4-6-2	EXJ	72A	70A	70A	71B	-	10/65	Rbt. 06/59
35006 Peninsular & Oriental S.N. Co.	MN	4-6-2	SAL	72B	72B	72B	70E	-	08/64	Rbt. 10/59
35007 Aberdeen Commonwealth	MN	4-6-2	SAL	72B	72B	72B	70E	70G	07/67	Rbt. 06/58
35008 Orient Line	MN	4-6-2	SAL	72B	72A	72A	71B	70F	07/67	Rbt. 06/57
35009 Shaw Savill	MN	4-6-2	SAL	72B	72B	72A	72A	-	09/64	Rbt. 03/57
35010 Blue Star	MN	4-6-2	SAL	70A	70A	71B	72A	70F	09/66	Rbt. 01/57
35011 General Steam Navigation	MN	4-6-2	9E	70A	70A	72A	71B	70F	02/66	Rbt. 07/59
35012 United States Lines	MN	4-6-2	9E	70A	70A	70A	70A	70G	04/67	Rbt. 03/57
35013 Blue Funnel	MN	4-6-2	9E	70A	72A	72A	72A	70F	07/67	Rbt. 05/56
35014 Nederland Line	MN	4-6-2	9E	70A	71B	70A	70A	70G	03/67	Rbt. 07/56
35015 Rotterdam Lloyd	MN	4-6-2	9E	70A	70A	73A	70A	-	02/64	Rbt. 06/58
35016 Elders Fyffes	MN	4-6-2	9E	70A	70A	70A	70A	-	08/65	Rbt. 04/57
35017 Belgian Marine	MN	4-6-2	9E	70A	70A	70A	70A	70G	07/66	Rbt. 04/57
35018 British India Line	MN	4-6-2	9E	70A	70A	70A	70A	-	08/64	Rbt. 02/56
35019 French Line CGT	MN	4-6-2	9E	70A	70A	70A	70A	-	09/65	Rbt. 05/59
35020 Bibby Line	MN	4-6-2	9E	70A	70A	70A	70A	-	02/65	Rbt. 04/56
35021 New Zealand Line	MN	4-6-2	09/48	70A	70A	71B	71B	-	08/65	Rbt. 06/59
35022 Holland America Line	MN	4-6-2	10/48	RTS	71B	71B	72A	70G	05/66	Rbt. 06/56
35023 Holland Afrika Line	MN	4-6-2	11/48	72A	72A	72A	71B	70F	07/67	Rbt. 02/57
35024 East Asiatic Company	MN	4-6-2	11/48	72A	72A	72A	70A	-	01/65	Rbt. 05/59
35025 Brocklebank Line	MN	4-6-2	11/48	72A	70A	71B	72A	-	09/64	Rbt. 12/56
35026 Lamport & Holt Line	MN	4-6-2	12/48	73A	73A	71B	72A	70G	03/67	Rbt. 01/57
35027 Port Line	MN	4-6-2	12/48	73A	73A	71B	71B	70F	09/66	Rbt. 05/57
35028 Clan Line	MN	4-6-2	12/48	73A	73A	73A	70A	70G	07/67	Rbt. 11/59
35029 Ellerman Lines	MN	4-6-2	02/49	74C	74C	70A	70A	70G	09/66	Rbt. 09/59
35030 Elder Dempster Lines	MN	4-6-2	04/49	74C	74C	70A	70A	70G	07/67	Rbt. 04/58

Number	Class	W.Arrgt.	1950	W/drawn	Notes
36001	Leader	0-6-6-0	06/49	11/50	Withdrawn & broken up after trials. Not allocated to a Depot.
36002	"	"	-	n/a	Completed, but never used.
36003	"	"	-	n/a	Part built
36004	"	"	-	n/a	Part built
36005	"	"	-	n/a	Frames laid
36006	"	"	-	n/a	Preparatory work done

Number	Class	W.Arrgt.	1948	w/drawn	Notes
K.E.S.R. No.4	L.S.W.R. 0330	0-6-0ST	KESR	08/48	Not allocated a B.R. Number

ISLE OF WIGHT LOCOMOTIVES

Number & Name		Class	W. A.	1948	1952	1955	1959	1963	1966	w/dwn	Notes
W1	Medina	E1	0-6-0T	NPT	71E	70G	-	-	-	04/57	
W2	Yarmouth	E1	0-6-0T	NPT	71E	70G	-	-	-	10/56	
W3	Ryde	E1	0-6-0T	NPT	71E	70G	70H	-	-	07/59	
W4	Wroxall	E1	0-6-0T	NPT	71E	70G	70H	-	-	11/60	
W8	Freshwater	A1X	0-6-0T	NPT	-	-	-	-	-	09/49	became 32646 09/49
W13	Carisbrooke	A1X	0-6-0T	NPT	-	-	-	-	-	09/49	became 32677 09/49
W14	Fishbourne	O2	0-4-4T	RYD	71F	70H	70H	70H	70H	01/67	
W15	Cowes	O2	0-4-4T	RYD	71F	70H	-	-	-	06/56	
W16	Ventnor	O2	0-4-4T	RYD	71F	70H	70H	70H	70H	01/67	
W17	Seaview	O2	0-4-4T	RYD	71F	70H	70H	70H	70H	01/67	
W18	Ningwood	O2	0-4-4T	RYD	71F	70H	70H	70H	-	12/65	
W19	Osborne	O2	0-4-4T	RYD	71F	70H	-	-	-	12/55	
W20	Shanklin	O2	0-4-4T	RYD	71F	70H	70H	70H	70H	01/67	
W21	Sandown	O2	0-4-4T	RYD	71F	70H	70H	70H	70H	05/66	
W22	Brading	O2	0-4-4T	RYD	71F	70H	70H	70H	70H	01/67	
W23	Totland	O2	0-4-4T	RYD	71F	70H	-	-	-	09/55	
W24	Calbourne	O2	0-4-4T	RYD	71F	70H	70H	70H	70H	03/67	
W25	Godshill	O2	0-4-4T	NPT	71F	70G	70H	-	-	12/62	
W26	Whitwell	O2	0-4-4T	NPT	71E	70G	70H	70H	70H	05/66	
W27	Merstone	O2	0-4-4T	NPT	71E	70G	70H	70H	70H	01/67	
W28	Ashey	O2	0-4-4T	NPT	71E	70G	70H	70H	70H	01/67	
W29	Alverstone	O2	0-4-4T	NPT	71E	70G	70H	70H	70H	05/66	
W30	Shorwell	O2	0-4-4T	NPT	71E	70G	70H	70H	-	09/65	
W31	Chale	O2	0-4-4T	NPT	71E	70G	70H	70H	70H	03/67	
W32	Bonchurch	O2	0-4-4T	NPT	71E	70G	70H	70H	-	10/64	
W33	Bembridge	O2	0-4-4T	NPT	71E	70G	70H	70H	70H	01/67	
W34	Newport	O2	0-4-4T	NPT	71E	70G	-	-	-	09/55	
W35	Freshwater	O2	0-4-4T	-	71E	70G	70H	70H	70H	10/66	was 30181 until 04/49
W36	Carisbrooke	O2	0-4-4T	-	71E	70G	70H	70H	-	06/64	was 30198 until 04/49

DEPARTMENTAL LOCOMOTIVES

Number	Class	W.Arrgt.	Normal Location	w/dwn	Notes
77S	C14	0-4-0T	Redbridge Sleeper Works	04/59	
DS233	USA	0-6-0T	Redbridge Sleeper Works	03/67	renumbered from 30061 10/62
DS234	USA	0-6-0T	Meldon Quarry	03/67	renumbered from 30062 12/62
DS235	USA	0-6-0T	Lancing Carriage Works	08/65	renumbered from 30066 03/63
DS236	USA	0-6-0T	Lancing Carriage Works	08/65	renumbered from 30074 03/63
DS237	USA	0-6-0T	Ashford Wagon Works	09/67	named MAUNSELL - renumbered from 30065 11/63
DS238	USA	0-6-0T	Ashford Wagon Works	09/67	named WAINWRIGHT - renumbered from 30070 08/63
DS239	C	0-6-0	Ashford Wagon Works	10/66	renumbered from 31592 07/63
DS240	C	0-6-0	Ashford Wagon Works	10/66	renumbered from 31271 07/63
DS377	A1X	0-6-0T	Brighton Works	05/62	became 32635 03/59 Stroudley Yellow Livery
DS515	A1X	0-6-0T	Lancing Carriage Works	11/53	became 32650 11/53
DS680	A1	0-6-0T	Lancing Carriage Works	06/62	Was S.R. No. 680S. Renumbered 11/50
DS681	A1X	0-6-0T	Lancing Carriage Works	06/63	renumbered from 32659 08/53
DS682	G6	0-6-0T	Meldon Quarry	12/62	renumbered from 30238 11/60
DS3152	G6	0-6-0T	Meldon Quarry	08/60	renumbered from 30272 06/50
DS3191	A12	0-4-2	Eastleigh	11/51	renumbered from (30)612 04/51
500S	T	0-6-0T	Meldon Quarry	11/49	
700S	D1M	0-4-2T	Eastleigh	05/49	700S & 701S were fitted with oil pumping
701S	D1M	0-4-2T	Fratton	12/51	equipment for fuelling locos temporarily converted in the late 1940s to oil burners.